What Use Is Sociology?

What Use Is Sociology?

Zygmunt Bauman

Conversations with
Michael Hviid Jacobsen and Keith Tester

polity

First published in 2014 by Polity Press

Polity Press
65 Bridge Street
Cambridge CB2 1UR, UK

Polity Press
350 Main Street
Malden, MA 02148, USA

ISBN-13: 978-0-7456-7124-6
ISBN-13: 978-0-7456-7125-3(pb)

A catalogue record for this book is available from the British Library.

Typeset in 11 on 14pt Sabon by
Servis Filmsetting Ltd, Stockport, Cheshire
Printed and bound in Great Britain by T.J. International Ltd, Padstow, Cornwall

For further information on Polity, visit our website: www.politybooks.com

Contents

Preface   vii

Introduction   1

1   What is sociology?   7

2   Why do sociology?   35

3   How to do sociology?   67

4   What does sociology achieve?   105

Preface

This little book seeks to encourage sociologists to identify themselves as the active subjects of a way of addressing the world rather than the value-free technicians of an alleged science. The text consists of four conversations with Zygmunt Bauman, carried out between January 2012 and March 2013, combined with responses to questions, recordings of personal meetings between the three of us, letters and fragments from a couple of texts Bauman has published in less accessible outlets. The material has been arranged into loosely thematic strands in order to establish continuities, resonances and, sometimes, to leave threads deliberately dangling. We have tidied up the grammar where necessary (written English is, we noticed, often very different from spoken English and the latter sometimes looks extremely clumsy on the page) but deliberately done little else to the material. The aim has been to inspire a conversation going beyond the conversations in the book.

The intention is that the book will be used by current and future sociologists to encourage fresh reflection about what we do, why, how and who it is for. It is also an example of a possible different way of writing sociology. The form and content of the book go together. Throughout the aim is to encourage sociologists to apply to our own practice the moral and political message of Bauman's work: there is an alternative but it is up to us to make it.

Michael Hviid Jacobsen and Keith Tester

the less managerial, even anti-managerial, more traditional, humanistic variation of sociology ... aims at making human behaviour less predictable by activating inner, motivational sources of decision – supplying human beings with ampler knowledge of their situation and so enlarging the sphere of their freedom of choice.

Zygmunt Bauman in the *Polish Sociological Bulletin*, 1967

more than ever we must beware of falling into the traps of fashions which may well prove more detrimental than the malaise they claim to cure. Well, our vocation, after all these unromantic years, may become again a testfield of courage, consistency, and loyalty to human values.

We would be well advised if we carved on the walls of our sociological lecture rooms what Max Weber said more than half a century ago: 'If the professional thinker has an immediate obligation at all, it is to keep a cool head in the face of the idols prevailing at the time, and if necessary to swim against the stream.'

Zygmunt Bauman, Inaugural Lecture, University of Leeds, 1972

Introduction

The raw stuff processed by the sociological imagination is human experience. The end-product of the sociological imagination called 'social reality' is cast of the metal smelted from the ore of experience. Though its chemical substance cannot but reflect the composition of the ore, the product's content also bears the mark of the smelting process which divides the ore's ingredients into useful product and waste, while its shape depends on the mould (that is, the cognitive frame) into which the melted metal has been poured.

Zygmunt Bauman, *Society under Siege*, 2002

There are many different, constantly changing, ever expanding and mutually conflicting uses of sociology. This makes the question of the 'use of sociology' continuously relevant and pertinent.[1] Moreover, the question 'What use is sociology?' is particularly worth asking because sociology is different from almost any other

---

[1] See, for example, Paul F. Lazarsfeld, William H. Sewell and Harold L. Wilensky (eds), *The Uses of Sociology* (New York: Basic Books, 1967).

Introduction

area of intellectual work. Whereas most can identify an object 'out there' which it is their concern to investigate, sociology cannot. Sociology is itself part and parcel of the social world it seeks to explore. It is part of a social world in truth capable of carrying on without the insights of sociology.

There is a long standing tradition, and lots of current practice, which sees this situation as terrible and to be overcome at all costs. Various attempts have been – and are – made to put a barrier between sociology and the social world. There has been – and still is – a constant fetishization of methodology, a stress on 'value neutrality', the development of a specialized and esoteric 'scientific' language designed to confuse the uninitiated, the adoption of the paraphernalia of professionalism – all of which function as a barrier between sociology and the world it investigates. In this way, sociology becomes some kind of scientific 'sorcery' that takes on a life of its own far removed and isolated from the life of the human beings it pretends to describe, investigate and analyse.[2] Sociology inside this barrier is said to be scientific and objective because, unlike every social activity sociologists explore, it is pretended to be uniquely free of power, self-interest and bias. The sociologists who seek to hide behind the barricades then attempt to sell their insights – or wait to be bought by power through research grants – on account of their willingness to march to the passing bells of policy-makers. The business of putting sociology into social life is then handed over to others. The result of all of this desperate

[2] Stanislav Andreski, *Social Sciences as Sorcery* (Harmondsworth: Penguin Books, 1974).

denial of the status of sociology as an integral part of the social world it seeks to explore has been little more than the decadence of introspection, a banality of 'findings', an ideology hiding beneath terminology and last but not least a seduction by power. The result has been, in a word, *irrelevance*. The world carries on, sociology carries on, and rarely do they ever meet.

As a consequence, sociology needs to be rescued from sociology. This has been known since the late 1950s. American sociologist C. Wright Mills famously separated the sociological imagination from sociology and showed how the practice of the latter has absolutely no necessary connection with the former. Mills made an irrefutable case for the pursuit of a sociological imagination seeking to engage in a conversation with men and women. This conversation would be concerned to show how 'personal troubles' are inextricably linked with 'public issues'. The sociological imagination makes the personal political. It was no coincidence that Mills lined up the practice of the sociological imagination alongside the work of people like novelists and journalists. For Mills, the sociological imagination – like novels and journalism – enables the development of a 'quality of mind' enabling men and women to understand and to narrate what is happening to them, what they feel and aspire towards. Sociology bereft of the sociological imagination can only provide information, and, as Mills saw, the world already has more information than it can deal with. The world has grown thin in stories, not information, and where stories are thin so too is the ability of men and women to make sense of their lives in its broader historical context. Then they, in Mills's words, feel trapped. It is thus the job of the sociological imagination to show how personal life and individual biography is intimately connected with historical events and structural processes. It is the job of the sociological imagination to help people 'understand the meaning of their epoch for their own lives', and it is the ambition of the sociological imagination, according to Mills, to 'make a difference in the quality of human life in our time'.[3]

The practice of the sociological imagination thus makes demands upon the practitioner. First of all, it is necessary to develop an account of the 'epoch'. This account acts as the context in which men and women act. In the style of Honoré de Balzac it can intrude as an overwhelming presence in the lives of the characters or, as in Anton Chekhov, it can be quieter. But, nevertheless, the sociological imagination – with its concern to enable men and women to navigate in and understand the meaning of their historical epoch – requires an account of the context in which they live. The purpose of this account is to constitute a context for understanding, and therefore it has to have the facility to allow narratives to multiply. The measure of the validity of these narratives, as indeed of the account of the context, is the extent to which they resonate with historically lived experience. The criteria of validity are not quantitative or informational; they are narrative and experiential.

Second, the practice of the sociological imagination demands alertness to the lives of men and women. Here the generality of the account of the epoch has to be connected with a fine-grained particularizing awareness

---

[3] C. Wright Mills, *The Sociological Imagination* (Harmondsworth: Penguin Books, 1970), pp. 11 and 226. Mills's book was first published in 1959.

of the lives of men and women. One way of achieving this awareness is to consume popular cultural products, since they are popular precisely because they deal with, or compensate for, the experiences of daily life. While the domination of information might have caused the world to become thin in stories, the work of the culture industries has surrounded lived experience with a surplus of stories. The successful stories in the marketplace are those speaking to general yet experientially particular anxieties, hopes and aspirations. If they did not so speak, they would not be popular. The practice of the sociological imagination requires an awareness of these popular stories of the personal issues of lived experience, and the construction of connections with the account of the epoch.

The necessity to develop an account of the epoch and an awareness of the cultural stories resonant with lived experience sets two traps. In the first case, the account might be so distant from experience that it seems meaningless for the understanding of lives. Meanwhile, an awareness of the cultural stories can too easily lead to a collapse of the sociological imagination into fandom and fashion. It is possible to identify corpses in both of these traps, and their avoidance itself makes demands on the practitioner of the sociological imagination. He or she must situate their work at the hinge between the account of the epoch and the lived experiences of men and women. The practice of a sociological imagination calls for work about connections, dialogues and conversations, not truths or monologues. This means work refusing to hide behind barricades and, instead, embracing its implication in the social world. You know you have encountered such a work when it makes you *think*, when it provokes, annoys or raises a smile. You know you have experienced such a work when you have a leap of recognition which is immediately followed by the broken fall of awareness. You know it when you read about *them* or *us* and discover something about *I*.

Inasmuch as sociology achieves all of this it is *useful*. It is useful to men and women who have troubles and problems they experience as their own but which are, in fact, often rooted in the public issues of the historical moment. Sociology is *useful* when it offers narratives connecting epoch with experience. Sociology is *useless* when it gives information and it is actively *dangerous* when it is sold to the powerful. Sociology is *successful* when it is taken up by men and women as a tool through and with which they can connect their lives to their times and appreciate how transforming the former means acting upon the latter.

The work of the sociological imagination of Zygmunt Bauman is *useful*. Is it successful? Will this book be successful? The answers to those questions remain to be known.

Michael Hviid Jacobsen and Keith Tester

I

What is sociology?

Michael Hviid Jacobsen and Keith Tester *Looking back at your own sociological trajectory, your work was initially inspired by Polish sociology in the 1950s and 1960s and after that your immediate sociological environment has been British sociology. How would you – in hindsight – say that these diverse sources of inspiration – Polish and British sociology – have inspired and shaped your own thinking?*

Zygmunt Bauman 'Looking back', as you've asked me to, I can hardly spot a watershed or a violent clash of 'sources of inspiration'. Taking off from Poland, I was already set on my sociological travels and landing in Britain did not cause anything like a significant shift in my itinerary. Separated from Poland by a linguistic barrier, 'Polish sociology' seemed a different universe, but please remember that the barrier was one-sided: English was then the 'official' language in sociology's realm and sociologists in Poland read the same books and followed the same caprices of fashion and meanders of interests as their workmates on the other side of the Iron Curtain. Besides, British sociology in the early 1970s was not exactly in the forefront of the worldwide trends, and for a newcomer from the University of Warsaw there was not much to catch onto; indeed, the discoveries made in those years in the British Isles were, in almost every respect, old and sometimes even outdated stuff around the Vistula. Most of the excitements through which my British colleagues were to go in my presence (such as the discoveries of Gramsci, the Frankfurt School, 'culturology', hermeneutics, the nonentity of 'structural functionalism' and the greatness of structuralism, etc.) I had already gone through in the company of my Polish colleagues well before landing in Britain. To cut a long story short, my first decade in Britain might have been full of sound and fury, for quite a few reasons (and indeed it was, as I confessed to Keith Tester quite a long while ago), but however, that signified pretty little for my vision of the sociological vocation.

You have always defined sociology as a 'conversation with human experience'. This raises two questions. First of all, what do you mean by 'human experience'?

I mean both *Erfahrungen* and *Erlebnisse*: the two different phenomena generated at the person/world interface, which Germans distinguish and set apart yet English speakers, due to the lack of distinct names, usually blend in one notion of 'experience'. *Erfahrung* is what *happens to me* when interacting with the world; *Erlebnis* is 'what *I live through*' in the course of that encounter – the joint product of my perception of the happening(s) and my effort to absorb it and render it intelligible. *Erfahrung* can, and does, make a bid for the status of objectivity (supra – or interpersonality), whereas *Erlebnis* is evidently and overtly, explicitly subjective; and so, with a modicum of simplification, we may translate these concepts into English as, respectively, objective and subjective aspects of experience; or, adding a pinch of interpretation, actor-unprocessed and actor-processed experience. The first may be presented as a report from the world external to the actor; the second, coming from the actor's 'inside' and concerning private thoughts, impressions and emotions, may only be available in the form of an actor's report. In reports of the first category we hear of interpersonally testable events called 'facts'; the contents of the second kind of reports are not testable interpersonally – beliefs as reported by the actor are, so to speak, the ultimate (and only) 'facts of the matter'. The epistemological status of *Erfahrungen* and *Erlebnisse* therefore differ sharply; a circumstance responsible for quite a few confusions in the practice of sociological research and above all in the interpretations of its findings. The reliability and relevance of witness-supplied evidence change with the object of the witnessing – and that applies to both partners in the ongoing 'dialogue between sociology and human experience'.

Second, in what does this conversation consist? How does sociology engage in the conversation, and what makes sociology worth engaging with? Why should non-sociologists read it?

Like all conversations, sociology engages in conversation with lay *doxa* – common sense or actor's knowledge. It involves passing messages that turn into stimuli that evoke responses which become stimuli in their turn – in principle ad infinitum. The transformation of messages into effective stimuli is mediated by reception, followed by sense-making, which involves as a rule a (selective) interpretation. In its sociological variety the conversation is aimed at the confrontation between *Erfahrungen* and *Erlebnisse*, thereby 'relativizing' the latter while aiming at widening, rather than narrowing and limiting the conversationalists' spectrum of choices.

In my view, the crucial objective of such ongoing conversation is in the long run the breaking of the widespread, perhaps even nearly universal habit of 'non-sociologists' (otherwise known as 'ordinary folk in their ordinary life') of evading the 'in order to' category of explanation when it comes to reporting their conduct and deploying instead a 'because of' type of argument. Behind that habit there is a tacit presumption, occasionally articulated though mostly unreflected upon and hardly ever questioned, that 'things are as they are' and 'nature is nature – full stop', and a conviction that there is little if nothing that actors – singly, severally or collectively – can change in nature's verdicts. What results is an inert worldview, immune to argument. It entails a truly deadly mixture of two beliefs. First, there is a belief in the indomitability of the order of things, human nature or the state of human affairs. Second, there is a belief in human weakness bordering on impotence. That duo of beliefs prompts an attitude which can be only described as 'surrender before the battle has started'. Étienne de La Boétie famously gave that attitude the name of 'voluntary servitude'. In his *Diary of a Bad Year* (Penguin, 2008), J. M. Coetzee's character

C. objects: 'La Boétie gets it wrong'. And he proceeds to spell out what was missing in that observation of four centuries ago which is nevertheless fast gaining consequentiality in our times: 'The alternatives are not placid servitude on the one hand and revolt against servitude on the other. There is a third way, chosen by thousands and millions of people every day. It is the way of quietism, of willed obscurity, of inner emigration' (p. 12). People go through the moves, obedient to their daily routine and resigned in advance to the impossibility of changing it, and above all convinced of the irrelevance and ineffectiveness of their own actions or their refusal to act.

Alongside the questioning of the worldview that underpins such 'quietism', the sociological variety of conversation aimed at the expansion of individual freedom and the collective potential of humanity pursues the task of revealing and unravelling the features of the world which, however deceptive and misleading they might be, nevertheless supply some grounds for a kind of worldview that sustains and continuously galvanizes the quietist attitudes. 'Relativization' aims at both sides of the *Erfahrungen–Erlebnisse* encounter: it is the dialectics of their interaction that could be called the conversation's ultimate objective.

Can you perhaps give an example of this?

Allow me to return for a moment to Coetzee's alter ego; once more, he hits a bull's eye when he points out that the popular and deeply entrenched

> figure of economic activity as a race or contest is somewhat
> vague in its particulars, but it would appear that, as a race,

it has no finishing line and therefore no natural end. The runner's goal is to get to the front and stay there. The question of why life must be likened to a race, or of why the national economies must race against one another rather than going for a comradely jog together, for the sake of the health, is not raised. A race, a contest: that is the way things are. By nature we belong to separate nations; by nature nations are in competition with other nations. We are as nature made us. (p. 79)

He continues: but in fact 'there is nothing ineluctable about war. If we want war we can choose war, if we want peace we can equally well choose peace. If we want competition we can choose competition; alternatively we can take the path of comradely cooperation' (p. 81).

Just to leave no room for doubt as to the meaning of his observation, Coetzee's C. points out that

surely God did not make the market – God or the spirit of History. And if we human beings made it, can we not unmake it and remake it in a kindlier form? Why does the world have to be a kill-or-be-killed gladiatorial amphitheatre rather than, say, a busily collaborative beehive or anthill? (p. 119)

Now this is, I suggest, a clinching reason why, as you ask, 'non-sociologists should read sociology'.

This immediately gives sociology a political edge. What is the relationship of sociology to politics?

Willy-nilly, by design or default, sociology is deeply embroiled in politics. In a conflict-ridden society like ours with its conflicts of interests and antagonistic politics, it is bound all too often to turn partisan as well. Its subject, after all, is the interaction of *Erfahrungen* and *Erlebnisse*; *Erlebnisse* are endemically partisan and so is the task of decomposing the deceitful 'objectivity' of *Erfahrungen*.

What renders sociology an intrinsically political activity is besides the very fact of offering a separate source and legitimation of authority, alternative to institutionalized politics. In our multivocal and multi-centred society this is not, however, the sole source of authority engaged in the competition with the political establishment – not to mention its only alternative. With state-run, state-originated and state-authorized politics chronically afflicted by the bane of ineffectiveness which is caused by a perpetual deficit of power – after a long period when it was the focus of genuine or attempted condensation and monopolization – the tendency nowadays is for a constantly widening spectrum of life pursuits to be spread all over the social body (recall Anthony Giddens's concept of 'life politics' as it takes over, or is burdened with, an ever growing number of the functions once embraced and jealously guarded by institutionalized, state-centred and/or state-oriented politics).

Is sociology an ethical practice and, if so, how?

As in the case of the 'political', sociology cannot help being ethical ('ethical *practice*' is in my vocabulary a pleonasm; ethics *is* practice – of articulating, preaching, promoting and/or imposing rules of moral conduct). Morality is an issue of responsibility towards an Other;

and the most powerful argument in favour of taking on that responsibility is the fact of the mutual dependency of humans, the condition which sociology explores, puts vividly on display and indefatigably hammers home. One lesson a reader of sociological treatises cannot fail to draw is the relevance of actions and inactions of others to their own condition and prospects, and the relevance of their own actions and inactions to the conditions and prospects of others; all in all, the responsibility we all bear, knowingly or not, for each other's conditions and prospects. Yet, let's be clear that responsibilities, whether or not they are evident and unquestionable, can be (and indeed are) as often *shouldered* as it may happen that they are *evaded*. The utmost I would risk saying is that while properly performing their professional job, sociologists are willy-nilly, by design or inadvertently, preparing the soil in which moral awareness may grow, and so the chances of moral attitudes being assumed and of responsibility for others being taken may be increased. This is, however, as far as one can go. The road leading from here to a moral world is long, twisted and full of traps – which, by the way, it is the sociologist's task to explore and map.

How does the conversation which sociology offers differ from other kinds of conversation such as literature, art, film?

The kinds of conversations you've named (and one could extend their list, as I believe all three of us would agree) are complementary, supplementary to each other and reciprocally enriching. They are by no means in competition (at least, there is no predesigned and unavoidable competition) – let alone at loggerheads or cross-purposes. Knowingly or not, deliberately or matter-of-factly, they all pursue the same purpose; one could say that they 'belong to the same business'.

It is true that alongside the proofs of consciously and willingly sharing in the same calling, one can easily find ample evidence of mutual suspicion and rivalry between them – in a form so common and so widely practised in our times of quicksand foundations, mobile signposts and fluid identifications: the form aptly called 'one-upmanship' ('up' in the league of prestige and the line-up for grants). This is a *professional* rivalry, however, a rivalry between *craft guilds* – though not between their strikingly similar *craftsmanships* and *vocations* (though all too often the clashes of interest between guilds are – falsely, as it were – represented as an incompatibility of their respective craftsmanships). As the great anthropologist Frederik Barth taught us a long time ago, boundaries are not drawn because of differences, but the other way round: differences are keenly sought, and usually found or construed as well as zealously recorded, because boundaries, once drawn, require fortification and legitimation. And to recall another of Coetzee's many insights in the *Diary*, this time inspired by René Girard's parable of the warring twins: 'the fewer the substantive differences between the two parties, the more bitter their mutual hatred' (p. 13).

Rivalry with other guilds is indeed in the nature of guilds, being as it were the paramount reason to construct, establish and fortify them. From the point of view of the recipients and users of their products, their services are anything but antagonistic, however. They are, I repeat, complementary and enriching to each other. Signs happily abound that a rising number of the practitioners of the conversational crafts are coming to understand and appreciate that these days; 'interdisciplinarity' is increasingly *à la mode* inside the walls of an academe ever less confident in the security and market value of its institutional boundaries. Let's hope, though, that the emergent 'interdisciplinarians' won't in their turn seek shelter in a guild of their own . . .

Indeed you often link literature with sociology – the role of the novel with that of sociology. Moreover, you have expressed intellectual affinity if not kinship with some of the great novelists of the twentieth century. Can you explain how the novel, or literature more generally, can enrich sociology and our appreciation of it?

In his book *The Curtain*, Milan Kundera writes of Miguel de Cervantes: 'A magic curtain, woven of legends, hung before the world. Cervantes sent Don Quixote journeying and tore through the curtain. The world opened itself before the knight-errant in all the comical nakedness of its prose.' Kundera proposes that the act of tearing through the curtain of pre-judgements was the moment of the birth of modern arts. It was a destructive gesture that modern arts have since endlessly repeated. And the repetition needs to be, and cannot but be, endless, since the magic curtain promptly sews back patches, glues slits and fills the remaining holes with new stories to replace those discredited as legends. Piercing the curtain is the main and recurrent topic of Kundera's book and the key to the interpretation of the history and the role of the novel, to which that book is dedicated. He praises Henry Fielding for aspiring to the role of 'inventor' in order to commit, in his own words, 'a quick and sagacious penetration into the true essence of all the objects of our contemplation' – that is the piercing of the curtain that bars us from looking into that essence. He also commends Jaromir John, the author of *The Internal-Combustion Monster*, published in Czech in 1932 (the title referred to mechanically generated noise, which John singled out as the devil running the modern hell), for 'not just copying the truths stitched on the curtain of preinterpretation' but displaying instead the 'Cervantes-like courage to tear it apart'.

Not unexpectedly if you know his 'topical relevances', Kundera focuses on the 'destructive gestures' of *novelists*. But the image of the 'magic curtain' and its tearing through strikes me as eminently appropriate as the job description of practitioners of the *sociological* vocation. It means piercing through the 'curtain of prejudgements' to set in motion the endless labour of reinterpretation, opening for scrutiny the human-made and human-making world 'in all the comical nakedness of its prose' and so drawing new human potentialities out of the darkness into which they had been cast, and in effect stretching the realm of human freedom and retrospectively revealing all that effort as the constitutive act of free humanity. I do believe that it is by doing or failing to do such a job that sociology ought to be judged.

Writing a novel and writing sociology are not the same. Each activity has its own techniques and modes of proceeding, and its own criteria of propriety, which set them apart from each other. But I would say that literature and sociology are siblings: their relationship is a mixture of rivalry *and* mutual support. They share parenthood, they bear an unmistakable family resemblance, serve each other as reference points which they can't resist comparing, and they are yardsticks by which to measure the success or failure of their own life pursuits.

It is as natural (as it is useless) for the siblings obsessively to dissect their differences – particularly if the similarities are too blatant to overlook and the affinities are too close for comfort. Both siblings are, after all, after the same goal – piercing the curtain. And so they are 'objectively' in competition. But the task of human emancipation is not a zero-sum game.

The last answer explains why you have said that the world of literature and fiction (more so than the sociological work of Talcott Parsons) have helped shape your own sociological imagination. You specifically mentioned the work of Honoré de Balzac, Émile Zola, Max Frisch, Samuel Beckett and others. You once said that all the books you wanted to take with you if you were to be marooned on a desert island were novels (by Robert Musil, Georges Perec and Jorge Luis Borges). There were no sociology books whatsoever. What is it that these writers and novelists are capable of doing that so enamoured and fascinated you in your formative years as a sociologist and how did their work influence the way you now think about and practise sociology?

If you are after the 'real life' truth, rather than 'truth' overloaded with the doubtful and presumptuous 'knowledge' of *homunculi* born and bred in test-tubes, then you can hardly choose better than to take a hint from the likes of Franz Kafka, Robert Musil, Jorge Luis Borges,

Georges Perec, Milan Kundera or Michel Houellebecq. And if you wish to cooperate with your readers in their urge (conscious or not) to find the truth of their own way of being-in-the-world and to learn about the alternatives which lie unexplored, overlooked, neglected or hidden from sight (which I believe is the sole effort which makes the vocation of sociology worthwhile), you need to address your messages to them, having formed your messages in a language they themselves deploy to verbalize their experience, and focusing on issues familiar and relevant to that experience. Failing in that vocation leaves a sole alternative: an offer to managers to assist them in rendering the managed docile by dehumanizing them. An offer as fraudulent as it is unappetizing, to be sure.

There is another reason to take advice from the authors I listed rather than from the likes of Paul Lazarsfeld, Talcott Parsons, or for that matter Barney Glaser and Anselm Strauss. An unwholesome and unwelcome side-effect of making a statistically concocted *homunculi* the staple product of current sociological practices is a trained incapacity to grasp humans in their mind-bogglingly complex entirety (instead of representing them as aggregates of spare parts and aspects) and to grasp social processes in their dialectics and dynamics (instead of representing them as a concatenation of the power pressures currently in the limelight).

Indeed, resorting to fiction may be an important source of creative inspiration for many social thinkers and intellectuals pondering and analysing what is happening 'out there' in the real world. When practising sociology, do you see fiction as playing a particularly important

*role in how we formulate questions, how we write our
texts, how we analyse phenomena and themes, how we
communicate to our readers, how we think of ourselves
as artistic craftspeople, or perhaps, all of the above? In
short, if fiction is valuable to the professional work of
sociologists (and not merely as an individual pastime),
then in what sense?*

Whether they like it or not, 'scientific' and 'fictional'
accounts (mind you, that selection of denominations is
already, *a priori*, prejudiced and pre-empts an answer,
and so is condemned by logic as the crime of *petitio
principii* – or mistaking what needs to be explained
for the explanation) meet and confront each other
on the same grazing territory: human experience.
Unfortunately the sociological discourse, being conducted worldwide mostly in English, uses a language
that unlike so many other languages collapses into one
the two fairly distinct and poorly coordinated phenomena that are distinguished, as we have already seen,
through the German concepts of *Erfahrungen* (standing
for 'what happened to me' – an 'objectifiable' aspect
of an event) and *Erlebnisse* (standing for the spiritual/
emotional repercussions of the occurrence or predicament – the subjective aspect, notoriously resistant and
never fully submissive to 'objectification' and given to
never being completely articulated). The absence of such
a distinction in common sociological discourse results in
a tendency to reduce the 'reality' under inquiry, one that
happens to be a human reality, 'lived' reality, and one
that cries out to be treated in a much fuller fashion, to
Erfahrungen – thereby impoverishing its understanding
and deforming if not downright falsifying its articu-

lation and presentation. A respectful attitude to the novelists' work may, it is hoped, vaccinate sociologists against that pathology and render them, if not immune, then at least wary of and alert to that menace.

Let's continue with the question of literature. In his book The Uses of Literature, *Italo Calvino suggested that there are different 'levels of reality' in fiction which make fiction not entirely fictitious, and that some sense of 'truth' or correspondence with reality might be found in works of fiction. The Danish social scientist Torben Berg Sørensen – after meticulously studying and scanning heaps of classical literature (e.g. the writings of Franz Kafka, Fyodor Dostoevsky and a varied selection of Danish literature) searching for hints and clues regarding how to understand and analyse the encounters between citizen and judicial system – concluded that 'it is meaningless to claim that a novel should be verifiable! . . . Literature does not necessarily create "truthful" knowledge, which means correct or detailed descriptions of objective, identifiable outer aspects of reality. Rather, literature goes behind, making certain sequences of action more likely, allows us to follow the person from the inside, while he is acting . . . Literature creates provocative knowledge – meaning knowledge that does not fit into existing schemas of thought. It raises problems and asks questions about that which exists. Is it really like this? Does it have to be like this?' Obviously, fiction is not, and hardly ever claims or pretends to be, or tell, the 'truth'. However, is there any 'truth' in fiction, as you see it?*

From all I know of Torben Berg Sørensen's work (and what I know I've just learned from you), I gather that he and I see eye to eye. And yet I'd go a step further and declare that in my view the semantic field of 'truth' and the 'pursuit of truth', veracity and verifiability, or for that matter 'truth versus untruth', are – to start with – wrongly selected for ruminating on science's and literature's love–hate cohabitation. The semantic field of monotheism versus polytheism (truth versus truths) is much more proper and suitable. Or, for that matter, one of fixing versus unfixing. Or one of tightening up versus taking apart an intentionally protective, though consequently disabling, armour. In the last account, to borrow from Milan Kundera: one of weaving and hanging a curtain before reality versus tearing through it.

Of course, there is a 'truth' *in* literature, but it is the truth *of* literature – as much as there is a truth *of* science, though it can only be the truth *of* science. In both cases, the truths we are talking about claim their truth value on the ground of having faithfully followed the prescribed procedural code. It is not a question of scoring in the same league of truth-seekers, but playing in different leagues for different trophies. And it is ultimately one's understanding of sociology's vocation that dictates one's choice, not the intrinsic superiority of rivals and competitors in the same race on the same running track.

Let us start out with a question intended to frame the direction of the subsequent interview. For many years – at least for a century and presumably even for much longer – the so-called 'science versus art' war has raged in academia apparently without any party in the struggle coming out conclusively victorious (although in many respects the 'science' party has been successful in claiming the upper hand). Looking at some of the most pertinent and perplexing questions raised by such a 'war' or discussion – is science better than the arts or vice versa, does science provide a more accurate and truthful description of the world than the arts or vice versa, is science more important to society than the arts or vice versa, should science receive better funding than the arts or vice versa, etc. – how do you suggest that we as sociologists should respond to or engage in such a debate? Would it amount to seeking to square the circle to position ourselves (un/comfortably) somewhere in the middle?

A recent illustration drawn from a bottomless sackful of self-confirming and self-refuting, while similarly truth-claiming prognoses: at the last Venice Biennale a Polish artist and animator, Artur Zmijewski, repeated Philip Zimbardo's famous experiment with randomly selected people randomly split into prisoners and prison guards. The original experiment brought horrifying results and had to be ended after a couple of days once it became clear that the 'prison guards' were turning into torturers and murderers, whereas the 'prisoners' were about to be recast as their victims. Zmijewski's experiment brought exactly the opposite ('encouraging', as they were instantly acclaimed) results: the two protagonist sides cooperated, in a spirit of mutual understanding, tolerance and solidarity, in elaborating a satisfactory, humane modus covivendi . . .

What jumps to mind in this context is the 'theory of human relations', now by and large forgotten, yet received as a bombshell in its time, which was based on Elton Mayo's Hawthorne studies conducted in the 1920s and 1930s at the Hawthorne works of the Western Electric Company, near Chicago. Mayo attempted to strip away one by one the coercive methods used to boost the discipline and submissiveness of the workers, and in this way their efficiency as well; contrary to every letter of received wisdom of his time, the efficiency of their work took off sharply and continued to rise. For the received wisdom, this was the most recondite mystery of them all (the canonical beliefs were grounded in the likes of Frederick Taylor's time and motion measurements and Henry Ford's conveyer belt, according to the practice of an industrial punishment-based regime).

In both the above cases, the surprise and bewilderment of the sages was a side-effect of what can be called their 'Cartesian fallacy': the tacit presumption of the neatness of the subject/object juxtaposition of the status of the researchers and that of the researched. It was a presumption debunked and swept away the moment the 'objects' of Zmijewski's and Mayo's experiments became aware of having been made co-players in an experimental game, flattered by the signs of public importance assigned to the game and the sudden attention from on high to what they were doing, and so keen to oblige by playing the game by the book and acquitting themselves as best they could of whatever the assigned role might have required.

Are more 'illustrations' needed? I believe not, as those two go straight to the heart of the matter. And the 'heart of the matter', in a nutshell, is the following: the truth produced with the help of the standards of science is grounded in the genuine or assumed applicability of the Cartesian subject/object dichotomy. In other words, it is valid in so far and only in as far as that dichotomy holds; it would therefore be valid in the 'human sciences' were their objects, humans, to be stripped of subjectivity – which they were not even under the most extreme attempts to strip them of it, as in Auschwitz or the Gulag. The obstreperous, indomitable and irremovable factor standing between natural-scientific and social-scientific truths is precisely the subjectivity of humans – and the ensuing *identity*, not the ontological and epistemological *opposition*, of the statuses of researchers and those they research.

The arts differ from sciences (including their 'social' variety) in trying to grasp the truth of their objects in their 'real life', not in conditions artificially simplified, reduced, 'decontaminated' and 'sanitized' by the 'ideal experiment' – and also and most importantly because of the fact that they are forced and doomed to treat their objects as *subjects*, that is to presume the identity of their own and their objects' statuses; if not for any other reason, then at least for the fact that, unlike neutrons, leucocytes or geological strata, their 'objects' are *choosing* creatures, and the social scientists' ways of putting things are factors in their choices. This circumstance alone already draws an unencroachable limit to some social-scientific dreamers of promotion to the natural-scientific status of authority and prestige. At least, that is, as long as they set their eyes on the natural-scientific example while turning their backs on writers and artists ... their dreams of 'maturing' to the status of 'natural' sciences are as idle and silly as they are suicidal for the social-scientific vocation.

Your work is often referred to or regarded as a variant of 'critical social theory'. Knowing that you do not venture into discussing such intellectual pigeonholing, we will refrain from asking what you think of such a label. However, Max Horkheimer once insisted that critical social theory had 'superseded theology but has no new heaven to which it can point, not even a mundane one'. So do we need critical social theory today – or do we instead need a new theology?

Sociology is a critical activity, in as far as it performs an ongoing Derridean deconstruction of the perception of social realities, followed by a continuous 'politics of campaign' (as defined by Richard Rorty) – whether or not it codifies that practice into 'theory'. Where it sharply differs from theologically inspired critique is in the *absence* of a pre-postulated – pre-designed or pre-anticipated – *telos*: of a model of 'good society' fixed in advance, viewed as a secularized equivalent/replacement of the 'Kingdom of God' which the kingdom of man strives to match. The sole attribute which sociological critique (perpetually unfinished and, similarly to Freudian psychoanalysis, unfinishable in principle) is ready to ascribe to the 'good society' is its implanted, persistent and inveterate self-criticism: its awareness, in perpetuity, that none of its current shapes is *good enough*, each given to, and yearning for, further improvements. If the 'politics of movement towards *telos*' (or 'politics of movement', as Rorty dubbed it) is bent on cutting down the number of outstanding improvements and narrowing down the range of postulated actions, a critique informed by a strategy of the 'politics of campaigns' neither desires such a reduction and such a narrowing down nor believes in their plausibility.

I am inclined to think that the question for liquid

modern life, incessantly and hopelessly hungry for interpretation, is not 'do we *need* critical social theory?': that
life, being nothing other than a continuous critique of
extant realities, gestates it incessantly, spontaneously
and on a massive scale. No reflection on that life can
possibly begin, let alone be seen through, without it.
The second eventuality you consider looks more intriguing; it shuns resolute answers. Though the true bone of
contention, I think, and a genuinely relevant query, is
not whether we *need* a 'new theology', but whether we
are capable of composing it, credibly. And how it would
relate to the experience of liquid modern life were we,
against all odds, to try to compose it.

*Continuing the theological theme: Sociology explores
troubles and issues; in many ways it can be understood
as a discipline which is about explaining to men and
women why they suffer, and how and why society can
be seen as the cause of their suffering. If this claim is
right, does it follow that sociology is in fact a secular
theodicy?*

Why *theodicy*?! Why turn to Gottfried Leibniz's clever
yet well-nigh universally ridiculed expedient, which was
meant to reconcile the irreconcilable: the omnipotence
and all-loving nature of God, with the all-too-evident
ubiquity of evil? 'Theodicy' means that this world
of ours, warts and all, is the best of the possible
worlds. Obviously (so Leibniz memorably suggested),
the apparent contradiction between the proliferation of
evil and divine *agape* has its roots in human ignorance
and incomprehension. The presence of evil in the world
acknowledged to be ruled by an omnipotent and loving

God must (mustn't it?) be *necessary for the world's perfection* – and one can only blame the feebleness and sluggishness of human minds for failing to embrace the grandiosity of God's design and grasp its logic.

Having unpacked that message and spelled out the reasoning underpinning it, Voltaire put the essence of theodicy thereby unravelled in the mouth of a certain Pangloss, 'professor of metaphysico-theologo-cosmolonigology' and 'the oracle' at the court of Baron of Thunder-ten-tronckh – as well as, let me add, the precursor and progenitor, as well as the inspiration from beyond the grave of Margaret Thatcher's creed of TINA (There Is No Alternative). Pangloss, wrote Voltaire, 'proved admirably that there is no effect without a cause, and that, in this best of all possible worlds, the Baron's castle was the most magnificent of castles, and the lady the best of all possible baronesses'. 'It is demonstrable', said he,

> that things cannot be otherwise than as they are; for all being created for an end, all is necessarily for the best end. Observe, that the nose has been formed to bear spectacles – thus we have spectacles. Legs are visibly designed for stockings – and we have stockings. Stones were made to be hewn, and to construct castles – therefore my lord has a magnificent castle; for the greatest baron in the province ought to be the best lodged.

Jokes and witticisms aside, sociology stands, stubbornly and emphatically, in rugged opposition to theodicy; you may say 'it is constantly reconstituted through the secular opposition to theodicy'. The sole significant exceptions to that rule that come to mind are the Soviet rendition of 'historical materialism' (or, as Herbert Marcuse disdainfully called it, 'Soviet Marxism'), and the monster-grand-theory of Talcott Parsons; both, not accidentally, short-lived and long since resting in the dustbin of history.

Sociology (willy-nilly, by design or default, as I go on repeating) is bound to sap the foundations on which rest the popular beliefs in 'necessity' and the 'naturalness' of things, actions, trends and processes. It unmasks the irrationalities that have contributed to their composition and continuation. It reveals the contingencies behind the ostensible rules and norms, and the alternatives crowded around the allegedly sole possibility (that is, the one chosen at the expense of all others). All in all, the métier of sociology is, to borrow Milan Kundera's allegory, 'tearing through the curtains' that hide the realities from view by covering them up with their fraudulent representations.

There is always a danger, of course, as Theodor Adorno kept warning, that in pursuit of the parsimony and elegance of its accounts (one of the guiding criteria of scientific perfection) sociological theorizing may ascribe to social realities much more 'rationality' than they in fact possess; and the 'rationality of the world', let's note and remember, is the modern (and secular) version of theodicy. The danger, no doubt, is there, the bait is difficult to resist, while the temptation to swallow it is built into the logic of scholarly endeavour – so that the unconditionality of the anti-theodicean stance is by no means a foregone conclusion (there is hardly any power-that-be that would not be able to find, produce or buy some practitioners of a sociological trade all too eager to prove its entitlement to the status of 'no alternative'). The threat needs to be remembered and the seduction needs to be resisted. But in the endemically multicentred and dynamic setting of liquid modernity, the chances of the success of the temptation to divert and corrupt the character (and so the social effects) of sociological inquiry are probably less than in the 'solid modern' past.

Picking up on that last point, sociology seems to find itself in an exceptional position. It is a discipline in an apparently perpetual state of crisis – a discipline constantly having to defend and legitimate itself, a discipline obsessed with discussing its very own raison d'être. Thus, more than half a century ago, the economist Fritz Machlup toyed with the idea of an 'inferiority complex' felt by many sociologists when compared to the more mature or paradigmatic natural sciences. Do you think sociology still suffers from such an inferiority complex? And if so, how may we cure it?

Like Fritz Machlup, I met with sociology 'more than half a century ago', but frankly neither then nor since have I found or noted sensible reasons to experience an inferiority complex. I guess it all depends on the criteria chosen for allocating a place in the league table, and on the league one believes oneself to be playing in. Machlup is known to cast knowledge as a money-making device, and I suspect that in speaking of an 'inferiority complex' he meant the inferiority of sociologists in the competition for securing funding, grants, plum jobs. If my suspicion is correct, then, for the sake of clarity, he would have been better to use the term 'relative deprivation complex'. However, I guess that it is not the notorious (and seemingly irreparable) bumpiness of sociology's road to riches that you are asking about.

Each of the three 'founding fathers' of academic sociology entertained different ambitions for the emergent discipline and sketched a different itinerary for fulfilling them. All were after the same objective: they wished to add sociology to the list of legitimate residents of the House of Solomon (as Francis Bacon chose to baptise the modern sanctuaries and repositories of learning which were aspiring to the collective management of human affairs). They differed, however, in how they justified the claim to residence. Durkheim averred that the realities sociologists are set to investigate meet the standards of realities explored by the 'established' academic disciplines boasting the most impeccable scientific credentials – there being therefore no reasons to doubt sociology's potential for turning out knowledge of equally unquestionable quality. Weber acknowledged the peculiarity of the realities scrutinized by sociology, but set out to prove that their particularity does not diminish the chance of investigating them with the same degree of precision as allowed by non-human (dubbed 'objective') realities. Simmel avoids being filed unambiguously with the advocates of either of these two stances. He just went on engaging, so to speak, in the dialogue with 'common sense' – in a kind of 'secondary hermeneutics' or 'second degree hermeneutics': reinterpreting what has been already interpreted, interpretation being the universal and only way of constructing the objects filling the human *Lebenswelt* (the lived world). Interpretation (both primary and the secondary) being perpetually *in statu nascendi*, and its finding therefore being barred from claiming a status more solid than that of an interim settlement, a 'perpetual state of crisis' is bound to be sociology's natural habitat: which, instead of giving reason for an 'inferiority complex', testifies however to the adequacy of sociological practice to the task it has set itself.

Rightly or wrongly, I count myself among loyal Simmelians. And so I believe that our job is not cognitively or pragmatically inferior to other jobs that are performed, intended to be performed or claimed to be performed inside academia. Like all such jobs, ours may be well or badly done – but in either case it needs to be measured by its own specific task-oriented criteria.

Remaining on this track and returning to the topic of 'science' versus 'art', and now with particular attention to its impact on the discipline of sociology and social theory, many have claimed that with the coming of social constructionism, deconstructionism and postmodernism, with 'narrative', 'rhetorical' or 'literary' turns within social theory, and with an accompanying fall from grace of realism, positivism and natural science trends within sociology, the 'science' part of 'social science' has increasingly – and to the detriment of the discipline – been diluted or downgraded. How do you see this?

You may easily gather my answers from our earlier exchanges. In my view it has been neither diluted nor downgraded. And most importantly, whatever has happened (is happening, needs to happen) is not 'to the detriment' of the discipline, and most certainly not of its prospective users. If it indeed happens, it will, if anything, signal and stamp sociological inquiry 'coming to its senses' and taking seriously the needs of the only public that needs the kind of services sociology is capable of offering and the requirements of the only service it is capable of responsibly promising.

I would say: sociology can be downgraded only together with the degradation of the human condition. But then the aim of sociology I am postulating is precisely rendering that degradation impossible.

Within the last few decades, especially since the 1990s, sociologists in their analyses have been preoccupied with how to combine the micro with the macro, the subjective with the objective, individual with structure, and so on. Just think of prominent names such as Pierre Bourdieu, Anthony Giddens and a host of others. This in many ways reminds us of C. Wright Mills's classic endeavour in The Sociological Imagination *(1959) – his ambition to link 'societal issues' with 'personal problems' or 'biography' with 'structure' and 'history'. You have never positioned yourself in such debates over the analytical priority of the individual or the social structure. Reflecting on your own work, how would you position yourself and your vision of sociology?*

The love–hate relationship between micro and macro looked to me (and still looks, despite its many successively assumed or simultaneously paraded disguises) as old as sociology itself – and certainly older than its first straightforward methodological cum political articulation by Herbert Spencer. One can close one's eyes to its ubiquitous and irremovable presence in sociological inquiry, but one can hardly wish or argue it away. I believe that the history of sociology can be told as a continuous effort to make their relations less ambivalent and more, if not completely, translucent.

I do not remember being particularly excited by the desire to reconcile the irreconcilable or separate the inseparable: fairly early I accepted the endemic and unexcisable ambivalence of the human condition, the double-bind and the interplay between (as I called it in the *Art of Life*) 'fate' and 'character' – and I guess that I tried, for better or worse, to encompass the sociologist's task, articulated by Mills as one of tying together 'biography' and 'history', in the practice of 'sociological hermeneutics': deciphering human conduct as a continuous interplay and interchange between situational ('objective') challenges and human ('subjective') life strategies; a sort of interpolation of Marx's reminder that 'people make history though not under conditions of their choice' combined with the rider that those conditions are unanticipated sediments or collateral products of their history-making. Well, what I am speaking about here has at the utmost the nature of heuristic advice, recommendation or guideline, rather than of an algorithm, sought by quite a few sociologists as passionately and as vainly as the alchemists sought the philosopher's stone.

One can live with that quandary. As for sociologists, they can hardly live without it. I, at any rate, cannot.

2

Why do sociology?

MHJ and KT *Why did you start to do sociology and what keeps you so motivated?*

ZB I tried to explain that to myself and Keith already – in our conversation eleven or twelve years ago. Returning from war to a prostrated, devastated country, I decided to shift my youthful fascination with the mysteries of the universe to such time as the realities of human misery on earth had been attended to. Well, almost seventy years later that motivation has lost nothing of its topicality, while 'doing sociology' has long since turned into a habit . . .

You consistently and firmly identify yourself as a sociologist. Why is this situating of yourself and your work so important to you?

I find this sort of question most difficult – indeed, perverse and treacherous – to answer. I sniff the temptations and ambushes of ideological glossing, ego boosting, self-apology and many other equally seductive yet similarly undignified blunders lining up along the way to a proper (*both* truthful *and* sincere) answer. And, frankly, even in the most private and intimate of conversations – with myself – I have repeatedly failed to answer that 'why' question of yours in a manner that would satisfy me as well as being fit to be aired in public. You probably expect a noble, elevating, uplifting, inspiring and reassuring response; a response of the kind I feel inept to deliver. My answer is thereby bound to come as a disappointment to you. Since you, my dear and most respected friends, however press me to compose an answer, I feel obliged to comply . . . But don't say that you haven't been warned!

Honestly, my friends, I can't convincingly explain (to others and myself alike) *why* sociology is so important *to me*. All I can say is that I never learned any alternative way of living and so gradually I perhaps lost the curiosity, but also the ability and indeed the will, to try and taste other fashions of being-in-the-world. Or perhaps it is that after so many years of thinking it and practising it, sociology for me has become no longer separable from the rest of my life. It has stealthily acquired the status of 'normality' – a status known to resent, perhaps even be unable to comprehend being questioned. Recently, I came across a confession of José Saramago in which the kind of embarrassment similar to that which your question aroused in me had been articulated in what seems to me the best imaginable fashion – with a degree of clarity I personally wouldn't claim the capacity to attain. I promptly recorded my debt to the great Portuguese in my *This Is Not a Diary*, under the date of 11 September 2010. I believe that a quotation from that non-diary of mine is the sole sensible answer to your question that I can offer.

'Do we talk for the same reason we perspire? Just because we do?' Saramago asks. Sweat, as we know, promptly evaporates or is keenly washed away, and 'sooner or later ends up in the clouds'. Perhaps this is the fate for which, in their own manner, words are destined.

And then Saramago recalls his grandfather Jeronimo, who 'in his final hours went to bid farewell to the trees he had planted, embracing them and weeping because he knew he wouldn't see them again. It's a lesson worth learning. So I embrace the words I have written, I wish them long life, and resume writing where I left off.'

'There can be', he adds, 'no other response'.

So be it. . .

Saramago recorded these thoughts having turned eighty-six – one year younger than I was when I first quoted those thoughts.

In your inaugural lecture in Leeds in February 1972, you proclaimed the following wish for sociology: that 'our vocation, after all these unromantic years, may become again a testfield of courage, consistency and loyalty to human values'. Does this still apply to sociology today – and is this vision of the 'testfield', as you see it, anywhere in the offing?

To the wish, yes, it does apply – and fully; it feels as fresh and as urgent and imperative as forty years ago. To the practice, however – not very much; at any rate much less than it ought. The odds are simultaneously in favour of the wish and against the practice. The same world prompts the wish and piles up obstacles against acting on it.

One of the most formidable obstacles lies in institutional inertia. Well established inside the academic world, sociology has developed a self-reproducing capacity that makes it immune to the criterion of relevance (insured against the consequences of its social irrelevance). Once you have learned the research methods, you can always get your academic degree so long as you stick to them and don't dare to deviate from the paths selected by the examiners (as Abraham Maslow caustically observed, science is a contraption that allows non-creative people to join in creative work). Sociology departments around the world may go on indefinitely awarding learned degrees and teaching jobs, self-reproducing and self-replenishing, just by going through routine motions of self-replication. The harder option, the courage required to put loyalty to human values above other, less risky loyalties, can be, thereby, at least for a foreseeable future, side-stepped and avoided. Or at least marginalized.

Two of sociology's great fathers, with particularly sharpened ears for the courage-demanding requirements of their mission, Karl Marx and Georg Simmel, lived their lives outside the walls of the academia. The third, Max Weber, spent most of his academic life on leaves of absence. Were these mere coincidences?

For whom do you write? Do you write for an audience that you are confident exists, or is it an audience that remains to be made; a hoped-for audience? If you write for the latter – hoped-for – audience, how do you reconcile this with the pressures from publishers who want definite audiences?

I apologize in advance for the lengthy argument which is bound to follow your query – but this apparently simple question of yours can't be answered without looking back, in search of the reasons which caused such a question to be asked and an answer to it sought.

My generation witnessed a slow yet relentless decomposition of the 'historical agent', which intellectuals mindful of the 'organic' standards set for them by Antonio Gramsci's code of conduct hoped would usher and/or be ushered into a land where the long march towards liberty, equality and fraternity – adumbrated by the thinkers of the Enlightenment but later diverted into capitalist or the communist cul-de-sacs – would finally reach its socialist destination.

For at least a century, the prime intellectual choice for the role of the 'historical agent' of emancipation was a collective composed of the assortment of skills and trades summarily categorized as the 'working class'. United by selling their labour at a fraudulent price, and by the denial of human dignity that went together with such a sale, the working class was hoped to become the one part of humanity which, according to Karl Marx's unforgettable sentence, could not emancipate itself without emancipating the whole of human society and could not end its misery without putting an end to all human misery. Once it had been ascribed such potency, the working class seemed to offer a natural and secure haven to hope; it was a haven that was so much more secure than the faraway cities where the writers of early modern utopias used to place the enlightened despots legislating happiness upon their unwitting or unwilling subjects.

Whether or not the ascription was warranted was a

moot question from the start. It could be argued that, contrary to Marx's belief, the restlessness on the early capitalist factory floors was prompted more by the loss of security than by the love of freedom, and that once security was regained or rebuilt on another foundation the unrest would inevitably boil away, stopping well short of its allegedly revolutionary potential. Indeed, after a long period of initial unrest associated with the melting of pre-modern economic and social structures, there came the period of 'relative stability', under-pinned by the emergent, apparently solid structures of industrial society. The politically administered instru-ments of the 'recommodification of capital and labour' settled into being a constant feature of the capitalist world – with the state given the active role of 'pump priming', promoting and insuring both the intensive and the extensive expansion of the capitalist economy, on the one side, and the reconditioning and rehabilita-tion of labour through the multiple provisions of the social state, on the other. However harsh the hardships suffered at the receiving end of capitalist expansion, and however disconcerting the fear of periodic bouts of economic depression, the frameworks fit to accom-modate lifelong expectations and equipped with tested and trustworthy repair tools appeared firmly set, allow-ing for the long-term planning of individual lives, confidence in the future and a rising feeling of security. Capital and labour, locked in an apparently unbreak-able mutual dependency, increasingly convinced of the permanence of their bond and sure of 'meeting again and again' in times to come, sought and found mutually beneficial and promising, or at least tolerable, modes of cohabitation – punctuated by repetitive tugs of war but also by rounds of successful renegotiations of the rules of cooperation.

So a 'historical agent' had to be created because capital and labour were locked together, not pulling apart?

Frustrated and impatient with the way things seemed to be going, Lenin complained that if they were left to their own ambitions and impulses, workers would develop only a 'trade-union mentality' and so would be far too narrow-minded to perform their historic mission. What irritated Lenin, founder of the strategy of the 'short cut' and 'professional revolutionaries', was also spotted by his contemporary Eduard Bernstein, but viewed with mildly optimistic equanimity. Bernstein was the founder (with not inconsiderable help from the Fabians) of the 'revisionist' programme of accommodation, of pursuit of socialist values and intentions inside the political and economic framework of the essentially capitalist society, and of a steady yet gradual 'amelioration' rather than a revolutionary, one-off overhaul of the status quo. As events kept confirming Lenin's sombre and Bernstein's sanguine anticipations, György Lukács explained the evident reluctance of history to follow Marx's original prognosis with a custom-made concept (which, however, looked back to Plato's shadows on the walls of the cave) of 'false consciousness', which the deceitful 'totality' of capitalism insidiously promotes and will continue to promote unless it is counteracted by the efforts of intellectuals striving to see through the deceitful appearances into the inexorable truth of historical laws – and, after the pattern of Platonic sages, sharing their discoveries with the deluded cave-dwellers.

When combined with Gramsci's concept of 'organic intellectuals', Lukács's reinterpretation of the vagaries of post-Marx history elevated the historical destiny and so the ethical and political responsibility of intellectuals to new heights. But by the same token, a Pandora's box of reciprocal accusations, imputations of guilt and suspicions of treachery was thrown open and the era of the charges of *trahisons des clercs*, uncivil wars, mutual defamations, witch-hunting and character assassinations started. If the labour movement failed to behave in line with the prognosis, and particularly if it shied away from the revolutionary overturning of capitalist power, it was the intellectuals who had betrayed their duty or botched its performance who were to blame. Paradoxically, the adoption of such an unflattering view of themselves was, for acknowledged, aspiring or failed intellectuals, a temptation that was difficult to resist, since it converted even the most spectacular displays of their theoretical weaknesses and practical impotence into powerful arguments for reasserting their key historical role. I remember listening, shortly after coming to Britain, to a Ph.D. student who, after perusing a few of Sidney Webb's writings, hurried to proclaim, to the unqualified approval of the tightly packed seminar audience, that the causes of the socialist revolution's late arrival in Britain were all present there.

There was writing on the wall, which, if read carefully, would have cast doubt on the intellectualist conceit of the British 'New Left'; but the recently rediscovered thoughts of Lukács or Gramsci did not exactly help to decode the messages they conveyed. How to link student unrest, say, to the winter of discontent? Was one witnessing rearguard battles waged by troops in retreat, or the avant-garde units of advancing armies? Were they distant echoes and belated rehearsals of old wars, or signs and auguries of new wars to come? Symptoms of an end, or of a beginning? And if a beginning, then ushering in what? News from abroad only added to the bewilderment and confusion, as the announcements of 'farewell to the proletariat' drifted in from the other side of the Channel together with Louis Althusser's reminders that time has finally matured for revolutionary action. E. P. Thomson's enchanting vision of the immaculate conception or parthenogenesis of the working class met with a frontal assault from the *New Left Review*'s editors for its theoretical poverty (meaning, probably, the conspicuous absence of intellectuals in Thompson's edifying story).

Did you see this at the time?

It is tempting, but it would be dishonest and misleading, to claim one's own advance wisdom retrospectively, just as it would be unjust and not at all illuminating to blame those locked inside those fast-running affairs for their confusion. The impending end of the 'glorious thirty' (the three postwar decades were so named only after the end of the conditions for which they stood, and only when it became obvious that they had ended) threw the familiar world out of joint and made the tested tools of that world's scrutiny and description useless. The time of hunches and guesses had arrived; orthodoxies dug themselves into ever deeper trenches, while heresies, growing thicker on the ground, gained in courage and impertinence, although moving nowhere near to consensus.

So the explicitly pointed out or glossed over source of intellectual disarray was the apparent vanishing of the historical agent, at first experienced on the intellectual left as a growing separation from and breakdown of communication with 'the movement'.

It can be argued that in the wake of the process you've just outlined, academia and intellectuals retreated into their own world behind what might be termed a 'firewall of jargon'. The firewall made sure the theories remained valid even if they had little or nothing to say to lived experience. How do you see this?

As the theoretically impeccable postulates and prognoses were one by one refuted by events, intellectual circles turned ever more zealously and conspicuously to self-referential interests and pursuits, as if in obedience to Michel Foucault's announcement of the advent of the 'specific intellectuals' era. Whether the concept of the 'specific' or 'specialized' intellectual could be anything other than an oxymoron was of course, then as it is now, a moot question. But whether or not the application of the term 'intellectual' is legitimate in the case of university lecturers visiting the public arena solely on the occasions of successive disagreements over their salaries, or of artists protesting about successive cuts in the subsidies for theatre or filmmaking, one thing is certain: to that new, institutionally confined variety of political stand-taking and power struggle the figure of the 'historical agent' is completely irrelevant and can be dropped from the agenda without a guilty conscience and above all without the bitter aftertaste of a loss.

However, must the hope and the job of emancipation

follow the vanishing 'historical agent' into the abyss, like the sailors following Captain Ahab's beckoning? I would like to argue that the work of Theodor W. Adorno can be reread as one long and thorough attempt to confront that question and to justify an emphatic 'no' as the answer. After all, long before the British intellectuals' passions for a historical agent started to dull, Adorno warned his older friend Walter Benjamin against what he called 'Brechtian motifs': the hope that the 'actual workers' would save art from the loss of its aura or be saved by the 'immediacy of combined aesthetic effect' of revolutionary art. The 'actual workers', he insisted, 'in fact enjoy no advantage over their bourgeois counterpart' in this respect – they 'bear all the marks of mutilation of the typical bourgeois character'. And then came the parting shot: beware of 'making our necessity' (that is the necessity of the intellectuals who 'need the proletariat for the revolution') 'into a virtue of the proletariat, as we are constantly tempted to do'.

At the same time, Adorno insisted that though the prospects of human emancipation focusing on the idea of a different and better society now appear less encouraging than those which seemed so evident to Marx, the charges raised by Marx against a world unforgivably inimical to humanity have not lost any of their topicality, and clinching proof of the unreality of the original emancipating ambitions has not been offered thus far by a competent jury; and so there is no sufficient, let alone necessary, reason to take emancipation off the agenda. If anything, the contrary is the case: the noxious persistence of social ills is one more and clearly powerful reason to try still harder.

Adorno's admonition is as topical today as it was

when it was first written down: 'The undiminished presence of suffering, fear and menace necessitates that the thought that cannot be realized should not be discarded.' Now, as then, 'philosophy must come to know, without any mitigation, why the world – which could be paradise here and now – can become hell itself tomorrow.' The difference between 'now' and 'then' ought to be sought elsewhere than in the loss of urgency of the task of emancipation or a finding that the dream of emancipation was idle.

What Adorno hastened to add, however, was the following: if the world seemed to Marx to be prepared to turn into a paradise 'there and then' and appeared to be ready for an instantaneous U-turn, and if it therefore looked as if 'the possibility of changing the world "from top to bottom" was immediately present' – this is no longer the case, if it ever was ('only stubbornness can still maintain the thesis as Marx formulated it'). It is the possibility of a *shortcut* to a world better fit for human habitation that has been presently lost from view.

There are no shortcuts – but are there any roads left to the better world?

I would also say that no visible bridges are left between this world, here and now, and that other 'emancipated' world, hospitable to humanity and 'user friendly'. Neither are there crowds eager to stampede the whole length of the bridge if such a bridge was designed, nor vehicles waiting to take the willing to the other side and deliver them safely to the destination. No one can be sure how a usable bridge can be designed and where the access to the bridge can be located along the shore to facilitate smooth and expedient traffic. Possibilities, one would conclude, are *not* immediately present.

So where does all that leave the intellectuals, the guardians of the unfulfilled hopes and promises of the past, the critics of those in the present guilty of forgetting the hopes and promises, and abandoning them unfulfilled?

As Adorno repeatedly warns, 'no thought is immune against communication, and to utter it in the wrong place and in wrong agreement is enough to undermine its truth.' And so, when it comes to communicating with the actors, with would-be actors, with abortive actors and those reluctant to join the action: 'For the intellectual, inviolable isolation is now the only way of showing some measure of solidarity' with those 'down and out'. Such self-inflicted seclusion is not in Adorno's view an act of treachery; neither a sign of withdrawal, nor a gesture of condescension (these two are connected: 'condescension, and thinking oneself no better, are the same', he pointed out). Neither did it signal an intention to break off communication – only the determination to protect the 'truth' of the human prospects of emancipation against the threat of being 'undermined'. Keeping a distance, paradoxically, was an act of engagement, in the only form which engagement on the side of unfulfilled or betrayed hopes can sensibly take: 'The detached observer is as much entangled as the active participant; the only advantage of the former is insight into his entanglement, and the infinitesimal freedom that lies in knowledge as such.' The strategy of communication proposed by Adorno is one of a 'message in a bottle'.

The 'message in a bottle' metaphor implies two presumptions: that there is a message suitable to be written down and worthy of the trouble needed to set the bottle afloat; and that once it is found and read (at a time which cannot be defined in advance) the message will be still worthy of the finder's effort to unpack it and ingest, absorb and adopt it. In some cases, like Adorno's, entrusting the message to the unknown reader of an undefined future may be preferred to consorting with contemporaries who are deemed unready or unwilling to listen, let alone to grasp and retain what they have heard. In such cases, sending the message into unmapped space and time rests on the hope that its potency will outlive the present-day neglect and survive the (transient) conditions that caused the negligence. The 'message in a bottle' expedient makes sense if (and only if) the one who resorts to it trusts values to be eternal or at least to be of more than momentary significance, believes truths to be universal or at least not merely parochial, and suspects that the worries that currently trigger the search for truth and the rallying in defence of values, unlike fleeting 'crisis management' concerns, will persist. The message in a bottle is a testimony to the *transience of frustration* and the *duration of hope*, to the *indestructibility of possibilities* and the *frailty of adversities* that bar them from implementation. In Adorno's rendition, critical theory is such a testimony, and this warrants the metaphor of the message in a bottle.

What message is in the bottle?

In the postscript to his last magnum opus, *La Misère du monde*, Pierre Bourdieu pointed out that the number of personalities on the political stage who can comprehend and articulate the expectations and demands of their electors is shrinking fast; the political space looks inwards and is bent on closing in on itself. It needs to be thrown open again, and that can be done only by bringing 'private' troubles and cravings (often inchoate and unarticulated) into direct relevance to the political process (and, consequently, vice versa). This is easier said than done, though, as public discourse is inundated with Émile Durkheim's *prénotions* – the rarely spelled out and even less frequently scrutinized presumptions which are uncritically deployed whenever subjective experience is raised to the level of public discourse and whenever private troubles are categorized to be proc-essed in public discourse and rerepresented as public issues. To do its service to human experience, sociology needs to begin with clearing the site. Critical assessment of tacit or vociferous *prénotions* must proceed together with an effort to make visible and audible such aspects of experience as normally stay beyond the horizons of individuals, or beneath the threshold of individual awareness.

A moment of reflection will show, though, that 'to bring awareness of the mechanisms that render life pain-ful or even unlivable does not mean they are neutralized yet; to draw the contradictions into the light does not mean they are resolved'. A long and tortuous road stretches between the recognition of the roots of trouble and their eradication, and making the first step in no way ensures that further steps will be taken, let alone that the road will be followed to the end. And yet there is no denying the crucial importance of the beginning – of laying bare the complex network of causal links between pains suffered individually and conditions col-lectively produced. In sociology, and even more in a sociology which strives to be up to its task, the beginning is even more decisive than elsewhere; it is this first step that designates and paves the road to rectification which otherwise would not exist, let alone be noticed. Indeed, one has to memorize – and to practise the best one can – Bourdieu's commandment: 'those who have the chance of dedicating their lives to the study of the social world cannot rest neutral and indifferent before the struggles that have the future of the world as the stake.'

Now I can return to your question 'for whom I write'. . . But I guess it is no longer necessary, because the recapitulation of my generation's experience provides the best answer I can offer – if not for my practice as it has been, then for how I would dearly wish it to be. Perhaps I scribble messages destined for a bottle. Messages in a bottle have no preselected addressees (if they had, there would be no need to consign them to the waves), but I trust the messages to seek and find their targets, like 'smart missiles': to select from among the individual sailors burdened by our liquid modern society with the task of seeking and finding solutions to the problems confronts them with those sailors who might be eager to open the bottles and absorb the messages they find inside them.

The answers you've just given cast light on what you sometimes, fleetingly, call your methodology of sociological hermeneutics. What is sociological herme-neutics? You've also sometimes mentioned that you use a sociological 'sixth sense' – what is that?

My kind of sociology I call *sociological hermeneutics*. It consists in the interpretation of human choices as manifestations of strategies constructed in response to the challenges of the socially shaped situation and where one has been placed in it.

Human choices are no more determined – though no less either – than the moves of card players are determined by the cards in their hand. A placing in a situation manipulates the distribution of possibilities. It sets apart moves that are feasible from those that are not, and the more probable from the less probable. But it never eliminates choice altogether. Even such resourceful and acute dealers of cards as the commandants of Auschwitz or Kolyma and their hirelings never managed to achieve that. Human power means the ability to manipulate the probabilities of human choices. No known power is capable, however, of expropriating the human capacity to choose. By the way, this is the reason why sociology should abandon its ambitions to compose 'scientific predictions' and thereby claim fully fledged 'scientific' status; the irremovable human capacity to choose would see to it that the predictions never rise above the level of a calculation of probabilities.

By 'sociological hermeneutics' I do not mean a separate variant of sociological activity, an idiosyncratic style for conducting it, nor do I mean a self-contained school. Sociological hermeneutics is a postulate that the effort of understanding human realities ought to be made with sociological tools. You may say that I claim for sociology *as a whole* (that is, for the ongoing inquiry into the difference made by humans being simultaneously products and producers of social reality) the paramount, nay decisive role in the effort to understand and explain (which in the case of humans amounts to much the same) human conduct and the verbal glosses that precede or follow it. Or you may say that I do not propose to reform sociology through hermeneutics, but hermeneutics through sociology. The postulate of '*sociological* hermeneutics' demands that whenever we pursue the meaning of human thoughts or actions we ought to look into the socially shaped conditions of people whose thoughts or actions we intend to understand/explain. In other words, the hermeneutics of human conduct is primarily a sociological, not a semantic or philological operation.

This is, alas, a postulate much, much more difficult to meet that in the case of demands spelled out in most of the 'handbooks of sociological research' which are composed for the indoctrination of first-year students. The ways of proceeding in 'sociological hermeneutics' are vexingly resistant to codification; they refuse to be reduced to a finite number of algorithmic rules, fit to be memorized and followed with little hesitation and no guilty conscience thanks to the absolution from responsibility which is the meaning and the main attraction of the rule. Hence the reference to a 'sociological sixth sense' – in other words, to *intuition*, something akin to E. M. Forster's appeal of 'only connect', which cannot be assured of its correctness in advance, which needs to justify itself in a dialogue (or polylogue) – possibly in an argument with no visible end, let alone a resolution. This make the prospect of 'raising' sociology to the rank of an exact science rather murky – but then humans, the creatures who set the standards for the science they've invented and practice, are notoriously reluctant to submit themselves to their own demands.

In your Leeds inaugural, you stated that the mission of sociology was to give 'power to the powerless' and continued by saying that without this ability, sociology would have to accept 'its own powerlessness in under-standing the social world'. Do you still hold to this position?

Since I said that, I have found no reason to change my mind. If anything, I have found a host of extra reasons to hold fast to it.

In Terence Rattigan's classic play The Browning Version *from 1948, we encounter the main character, Andrew Crocker-Harris, who is witnessing how the subjects he has taught for decades – Greek and Latin – increasingly come under pressure from and are deemed irrelevant or outdated by the newly popular subjects of science and sports. Crocker-Harris, on his forced retirement towards the end of the film, dramatically states to the audience of colleagues, students and their parents: 'How can we hope to mould civilized human beings, when we no longer believe in civilization?' Sociology is increasingly growing old in a world – just like Crocker-Harris's – that valorizes the new and the fashionable. Does sociology still have the chance in contemporary liquid modernity to help shape civilized human beings?*

Yes, sociology, just like Greek and Latin, can be counted as a contribution to civilization, but not in the same way as Greek and Latin. And Crocker-Harris – like so many others watching with a mixture of bewilderment and despair the twists and turns in the mode of their contemporaries' cohabitation – might have written the obituary to civilization somewhat too hastily. The ends (of X, Y, Z, and whatever else – of history, modernity, class society, industrial society, reading culture and a reading public, books, the world itself) have been announced too many times in the course of my unforgivably long life for me to count them all. This is, after all, what could have been and needed to be expected of people living in an era of interregnum, as we have been for the last half-century or so – a time when, ever more blatantly and conspicuously, the old ways of acting stopped working, while new ones, better suited to the fast-changing scenery and its new challenges, had not yet left the design bureaus. But the 'civilized' part of human history was from the start, and will probably remain, a mixture of learning and forgetting. Very few of our contemporaries are fluent in Greek or Latin, fewer still can play the musical instruments routinely used to accompany medieval singing, and how many of us can make fire with flint and tinder? Acquiring new skills is well-nigh inconceivable without abandoning the old. To succeed in tackling new challenges – challenges no less demanding than the old ones yet starkly different from them – old skills will be of little help, and so new ones are called for. For Crocker-Harris, who dedicated his life to instilling awe and respect for the old, ageing and increasingly irrelevant skills, it was bound to be a sentence of personal failure and a wasted life.

But the vocation of sociology is to purvey *orientation* in an admittedly changing world. And that vocation can only be fulfilled through tracing the changes and their consequences as well as scrutinizing the life strategies adequate for dealing with their demands. I believe that a world requiring perpetual reorientation is a natural habitat for sociological inquiry and the services sociology can and ought to render.

But to what do we orientate? One might claim that a thoroughly individualized society – like our liquid modern society, according to your analysis – breeds a cult of individualized intellectualism. Today, it seems, very few readers, students and even scholars identify themselves with great paradigms or theoretical schools of thought, but rather seem to revel in the writings of individual sociologists such as, for example, Bourdieu, Habermas, Luhmann . . . and Bauman. Thus, your own name is sometimes even mentioned in terms of 'intellectual guru', 'academic superstar' or 'world-famous sociologist'. Why do you think we see this tendency today to idolize certain individual social thinkers?

It's not an affliction specific to sociology. On the contrary: sociology follows a pattern common to all branches of knowledge, to the mental maps of the *Lebenswelt*, to the structure of the *Lebenswelt* itself. A pattern whose brief history and emergent features I tried to capture and summarize under the heading of the progressive weakening or even falling apart of human bonds and the new fragility and ad hoc and avowedly temporary as well as increasingly short-term status of structures – indeed, of the very notion of 'liquid modernity'. The pattern in question manifests itself in the trends to fragmentation, episode splitting, deregulation, individualization, privatization and (yes!) personalization, affecting almost every area of human interaction as well as the currently dominant *Weltanschauung*, or worldview. The bottom line of all its multifarious renditions and applications, and perhaps their shared source and inspiration, is the discovery that among the entities currently discernible in the world of human experience solely the individual's corporeal existence (for most of human history and until quite recently the much bewailed and lamented paragon of transience, vulnerability, fleetingness, brevity and indeed inconsequentiality and vanity) has a rising life expectation and credible prospects that it will rise further. . .

When more than half-century ago I entered the fields of sociology and philosophy, I found them neatly segmented into plots bearing the name of 'schools'. There was historical materialism, structural functionalism, ethnomethodology, structuralism, analytical philosophy, phenomenology, existentialism, and what not – the number changed from one survey of the field to another, but the principle of its mapping remained intact and unquestionable. The chapters of textbooks of the discipline's history also bore the names of schools. Individual names differed in the sometimes sharply distinct biographical and bibliographic data of their bearers, but there were only minor variations, well short of iconoclastic, in their bearers' approaches and scholarly practices. I suspect that the field of a scholarly discipline appears to a present-day newcomer in a completely different light: a vast expanse with a lot of criss-crossing tracts, paths and gorges trodden in all directions by clearly distinguishable figures of more and less distinguished personalities, each busy in blazing a new trail rather than keeping to one already blazed. Histories tend to be similarly rewritten: the stories are no longer the stories of successive paradigms, essentially school accomplishments, but of paradigm-breaking, principally individual feats; not of 'schools', but of 'key sociologists' or 'key philosophers'. And what I am talking about now applies to all branches of science – and yet more generally to all areas of culture and the arts. As a matter of fact, even more generally than that: its traces are spattered all around our daily lives. No nook or cranny of our mode of being-in-the-world, however minute and isolate, is genuinely free of them.

I wonder about the phenomenon of Mark Zuckerberg, who presumed that all human concerns ultimately focus on the challenge of self-identification and all roads of the searchers and builders of identity lead back to the body and mind of the seeker, and who therefore initiated the 'Facebook revolution' that raised him to the status of a multi-billionaire in a matter of a few years. I ask myself: Would that phenomenon have been at all conceivable at the time of my youth (it is not the absence of computers then that prompts me to ask)? Had Mark Zuckerberg been born thirty or forty years earlier, had he been trained by his teachers to unctuously regurgitate and recite Jean-Paul Sartre's homilies or to reiterate after Michel Foucault as if quoting from Holy Scripture that 'the author is dead', and had he learned from the apostles of the church of the 'New Criticism' that it is downright silly, and disqualifying for a student, to connect artistic texts with any personal details of the author's life – would it have occurred to him that it is precisely the 'personal details' that make the author, and that therefore his young colleagues were bound to be itching to match the celebrated author's glory by making their own 'personal details' public? And in the utterly unlikely case that it would have occurred to that earlier-born Zuckerberg, would millions of active users have indeed leapt to his invention (or spoils of robbery, according to some) and would the billions of dollars have followed them? It was only in the course of the last twenty years, as for instance Sebastian Faulks points out in *Faulks on Fiction*, that 'far from being banned from comment, the author's life and its bearing on the work became the major field of discussion'. And, he adds, this watershed change 'opened the door to speculation and gossip. By assuming that all works of art are an expression of their authors' personality, the biographical critics reduced the act of creation to a sideshow.' I suspect (or rather I am sure) that only in the last twenty years could Zuckerberg have had his revelation and decided to carry his good tidings to his fellow students, with his fellow students prepared to follow the Master along the road he pointed out.

Are we sociologists much different from Zuckerberg? In his book Teachers, Writers, Celebrities *(1981) Régis Debray plots a history of the intellectual. He raises a cutting question: has the intellectual now become just one more celebrity. Is it down to the celebrities to change the world?*

It is not a question of becoming celebrities; it's a question of the kind of services supplied. I follow Daniel J. Boorstin's definition of the celebrity as somebody who is famous for being famous. So what he or she is doing doesn't really matter very much, especially any services apart from fun and entertainment. At best they are idols, but they are not authoritative, they are not coming here to instruct you, to teach you. At the utmost you may try to emulate them. For example there is Facebook, which is a poor man's substitute for a glossy magazine or peak-time television. So it's not a question of celebrity, it's a question of changing the public.

Why do sociology?

Today, there is a huge and rising mass of individuals tussling in the void stretching between individuality *de jure* and individuality *de facto*. They need our services. So it's not a question of being a celebrity, it's a question of speaking to them, and that's the vision of sociology I'm trying to uphold. Twenty or thirty-odd years ago, I completely stopped using sociological jargon because that jargon has been invented especially to keep the entry to sociology as closed as possible, to break communication and to set boundaries. But if sociology wants to be of relevance, then it needs to open itself to people and start thinking as it did when I was a student of sociology: that we are here to collect the evidence and engage in ongoing dialogue with experience and to try to help people in their fight against the double plague of ignorance and impotence. I think there's a great chance and it's very, very exciting and that's the kind of vision which is opening in front of us.

You are now the subject of at least three films, you attend award ceremonies and your lectures are widely available on YouTube. Are you now fated to play the game of celebrity?

Let me answer with a personal story. Having come to Oviedo to collect a Prince of Asturias prize, I practically incarcerated myself in the hotel for fear of the crowds waiting at the entry for my autograph. However the self-confinement only lasted until the Spanish national football team, the recipient of another prize, arrived. After that I was free to move around the town unmolested: all the autograph-hunters were otherwise engaged and none of them paid any attention to me.

Anecdotes aside, however, please do not confuse being *seen* – 'being a celebrity' (that is, being known for being known) without having any influence on the thoughts and deeds of those by whom one is known – with being *listened to*. The forte of Régis Debray's 'mediacracy' (a uniquely felicitous blend of the 'rule of media' with that of mediocrity) is to promote the first eventuality of the pair while stifling the second.

I have been racking my brain in vain to find a way out of the quandary. The *agora* of our times is filled to the brim with market stalls and only admits buyers and sellers of commodities. Information travels only when it is sold and bought. And if you wish to repair that sorry state of the *agora*, you must first gain entry. You have to be listened to if you wish to be heard. Gaining entry to the market stalls is hardly a guarantee of being heard. But it is, alas, its unavoidable preliminary condition.

A quotation from Theodor W. Adorno: 'Whoever thinks is without anger in all criticism. . . . Because the thinking person does not have to inflict anger upon himself, he furthermore has no desire to inflict it on others . . . Such thought is happiness, even where unhappiness prevails; thought achieves happiness in the expression of unhappiness.' Is your thought happy? Has it achieved happiness?

I am not sure about the relationship between anger and thought. Love–hate? The impossibility of cohabitation coupled (exacerbated? mitigated?) with the implausibility of separation? Or is it a prime specimen of Jacques Derrida's family of *pharmakons*?

I find a modicum of anger to be a supreme stimulus to thought, and its excess more like thought's funeral director. But at what point does the modicum turn into excess? I have also sometimes found thinking to be anger's most effective tranquillizer, yet at other times its most reliable fuel. But how to know when is which? Following Paul Ricoeur's suggestion, I'd say that if in its first stage thought leads to the rejection of intolerance (through refraining from marrying disapprobation to power) and so causes the fonts of anger to dry up, and proceeds to tolerance (that is, the voluntary asceticism of power and so the suspension of anger), it is thanks to the gesture of indignation that posits certain objects as intolerable (the 'intolerable' should not be confused with intolerance; 'intolerable' is the product of a Hegelian 'double negation' of intolerance; 'intolerable' is thinkable and comes into its own only *after* toleration's triumph) that it eschews the trap of indifference which can follow the unqualified victory of tolerance. And that indignation, at the summit of thought's progression, means anger.

I know we are moving on slushy and poorly signposted ground here. Maps are useless on quicksand. But there you are: wandering without Ordnance Survey maps is the fate which we have decided, joyously or with sadness, to recast as our vocation. Take it or leave it.

And does thinking make me happy? It would be dishonest to give a resolute answer, whatever it may be. One thing I am sure of is that thought finds restfulness the most unbearably tiring, and so repulsive, condition; and also perhaps a sign that the time for the last rites is approaching.

Why do sociology?

You are not restful. You write a great deal . . .

Writing is the only fashion in which I've managed to learn how to express my thought communicatively; and even that fashion I've only mastered well short of my own satisfaction. . .

Does your productivity reflect an attempt to keep the conversation going or, by contrast, is it an attempt to make the conversation happen? Put another way, is your productivity a sign of the presence or absence of dialogue? Or is it a more simple case that the sociological vocation makes us all Puritans, working hard in our calling, without ever knowing if we are destined for the secular salvation of being heard?

Brilliant observation! Yes, perhaps we are all Puritans now – though by decree of history rather than by choice. We can't be sure of salvation and of the shape in which it will come when (if) it arrives. But this only adds to the attraction of Jack Nicholson's attempt in *One Flew Over the Cuckoo's Nest* to tear a boiler out of its concrete casing and heave it up to break the iron bars in the asylum window. Jack was not mad enough to believe that he had enough strength to do it, but he wished to make sure that no one, including himself, could accuse him of not having tried. And as you know only too well, messages, however loud and bright, nowadays come with a 'use by' date printed or presumed, and vanish as fast as they appear. However you judge the civilization of excess and waste which uses excessive quantity to compensate for the deficit of quality, you need to follow the recipe given to photographers by George Bernard

Shaw (follow the example of the cod and hatch thousands of eggs so that at least one of them will turn into a mature fish) if you wish your message to be taken in before the bottle is recycled or goes into the refuse bin. To 'keep the conversation going' you have 'to make it happen' – repeatedly, untiringly.

And please remember that whereas Jack Nicholson failed, his Indian companion in misery, taking inspiration from his failed attempt, succeeded – and got free.

You are quite consistent in your position that sociology is a conversation with lived experience. From this it also follows that texts you write are dialogues with their readers. The texts are talking with the reader rather than at them. This attitude is similar to one outlined by Michael Haneke when he once spoke about the relationship he hopes his films have with their viewers. He said that he does not want to spoon-feed his viewers and he wants to give them the possibility of participating in the process of making the meaning of the film. Consequently he leaves things unexplained (exactly what is going on in The White Ribbon?*), lets some narrative points drop, shows some things without explaining them. Of course, this raises the question of whether sociologists should watch Haneke's films (short answer – yes), but it also raises a wider question about the relationship between the author and the text. Do you seek to give your readers the possibility of participating in the making of the meaning of your texts?*

Haneke also speaks of 'trying to rape the viewer into independence', echoing Rousseau's injunction to force *le peuple* into freedom. My belief is that freedom

starts with asking questions and ends with 'spoon-
feeding answers'. Maurice Blanchot famously dubbed
answers the curse of the questions: freedom ends once
the cause of questioning is proclaimed and accepted
to be open and shut – we are free as long as we go on
questioning and lose freedom once we stop. Sometimes
I suspect that questioning, produced on stage as a
drama of emancipation, is directed from the wings
by Thanatos – and that the role of question prompter
or question instigator, whether an artist or a critical
sociologist, is not so much to facilitate and smooth
the road to an answer as to lay bare the iniquity of
Thanatos' plot and wrench the direction of the plot
of the drama from his hands. My wish is to bring into
view the potholes, traps and snares with which the
road to the answer is spattered, and thereby to foil
the plot. *Toutes proportions gardées*, I suppose that
Haneke and I are in the same business: the business
of spurring readers to *think* and of immunizing them
against the allure of quick fixes.

*Haneke refuses to explain the meaning of his films. You
never respond to your critics, never say 'this is what I
really meant', never close down the meanings which are
read from your work. As you have said, they are messages in bottles and like all such messages have to be left
to fate and fortune to find their readers. Now, Haneke
once gave an answer to the question of why he never
says what he really means. He presented the answer as
a joke but was actually deadly serious. He said that he
doesn't know the answers to the questions his films raise
because he doesn't have a particularly close relationship with the films' author. Well, do you have a good*

relationship with the author of the books and articles written by Zygmunt Bauman?

I tend to agree with you: Haneke was in all probability deadly serious. In exploring the mystery of the human mode of being-in-the-world, there are no omniscient oracles equipped with a hotline to God. Neither is there anyone who manages to follow Plato's sages out of the cave of existence to witness the pure, unsoiled ideas point blank. And even if there were, they would have little of use to communicate to the rest of us, unre-deemable troglodytes, of which I am just one of the innumerable many (as, I suspect, Haneke deems himself to be too). Anyone who wants to empower instead of disempowering the spectator or the reader must start from being relevant to the experience of cave dwellers. This at least is what I mean when I consider and conduct my trade as a never-ending conversation with living experience. But I would go a step beyond Haneke's for-mulation, a step beyond 'giving the spectators/readers a *possibility* of participating' in meaning making. I guess that the task is to demonstrate that without their partici-pation the struggle against meaninglessness stands no chance. Let me add that I doubt whether even then the struggle will ever be ultimately won. This doubt is no cause for despair, though. It is, after all, precisely that struggle which constitutes the human, all too human mode of being-in-the-world.

Can sociology make people happy?

It can – if seeing through the world that we shape to shape our condition makes us happier than we otherwise would have been. By contrast, there is little chance of happiness in closing one's eyes or looking the other way. And a fleeting chance it is, like the one offered by inebriation or drugs – with a heavy price to pay, in the currency of frustration, at the moment of sobering up.

Has sociology made you *happy?*

A tricky question, if ever there was one – and impossible for me to answer. After all, I have been a sociologist throughout my mature life and nothing else. What comparison could I base my evaluation on?

But as to the question of whether being a sociologist makes for a happy life, I can only echo (*toutes proportions gardées!*) the great and wise Johann Wolfgang Goethe; when, close to my present age, he was asked whether he had had a happy life, he answered: 'Yes, I had a very happy life' only to add right away: 'Though I can't recall a single wholly happy week.'

3
How to do sociology?

MHJ and KT *We'd like to push you on something. One of the effects of your work is to make readers question what they previously took for granted and, indeed, what they previously valued. For example you strongly imply that the thrills of the one-night stand are unethical and bordering on the inhuman. Your work implies the devaluation of the values of men and women. Three questions follow from this.*

First: What is the position from which it is valid to make these claims? If we wanted to put it extremely brutally – why should men and women listen to you?

ZB As to the latter, 'brutal' part of your question, I have asked it myself many times, and go on asking it. The fact that 'men and women' – quite a few of them – do listen remains a puzzle, and I can only guess its causes. But let me admit straight away that 'listening' and hearing the message are two different things; and so are hearing the message and following the recommendations that follow.

I am not a moral preacher, though the question of morality (that 'moral law inside me' which Immanuel Kant picked up as one of the two greatest mysteries of existence), and particularly of the sources of its strengths and weaknesses, is to me an axis around which all other secrets of the human condition rotate. And so I am not in the business of a 'devaluation of values', or for that matter rewriting ethical codes. What I am trying to do, and doing within the limits of my alas modest abilities (which means stopping well short of what could and should be done), is to articulate the values 'men and women' tend to follow while seldom articulating them and all too often articulating them wrongly when they are pressed to name them. And I try to do it in order to present those 'men and women' with dilemmas they confront in their choices but may fail to note – and so to enable them to make *their* choices with somewhat more awareness of what they are about to gain and what to surrender. And so, rightly or wrongly, I explain to myself their interest (as suggested by the translation of my writings into thirty-five languages) with a surmise that the dilemmas I sketch chime in with their lived-through experience and so might even be found helpful in making their choices. I try to give each of the alternative choices its fair crack of the whip. My intention, at any rate, is not to *evaluate* their choices, but to assist the choosers in evaluating them *realistically*, without leaving the moral significance of their choices out of the calculation. Of course, the road from intentions to their fulfilment is notoriously rough and bumpy and I wouldn't swear that I've achieved, or indeed can achieve, the effect I desire.

And as to the first part of your question, concerning

'the position from which it is valid' to do what I am trying, for better or worse, to do: I guess that it is not different from positions from which sociological claims are normally made – close observation of human conduct, empathy with actors' experience, scrutiny of the options their situation allows or does not allow them to take, collating and juxtaposing their perception of the situation as manifested in their choices with what is known of the circumstances determining (or more correctly enhancing or diminishing the probability of) their choices. It is taking that position that permits, and encourages as well as demands, one to voice such claims.

Second: Why should we start asking questions about ourselves, our practices, our lives? Here we're reminded of George Orwell's rebuke to those who wanted to transform working-class diets in the 1930s. He pointed out that if you've worked hard all day and been made to do things you'd prefer not to do, all you want is comfort food, and whether or not it is healthy just doesn't matter. What's so wrong with a life that does not ask questions of itself?

Well, to start with, it is not 'self-questioning' that Orwell had in mind. What he objected to was the *imposition* of views arrived at, embraced and promoted *without* taking the position we've just discussed: without scrutiny, knowledge and understanding of the situation of another on whom those views were imposed. Those who 'wanted to transform working-class diets' were not themselves working class, and Orwell castigated them for understanding little or nothing about the working-class situation and making little or no effort to put themselves 'into working-class shoes'. Orwell was up in arms against a society living under the threat and in fear of (in his own words) 'a soldier's boot trampling down the human face'; a society incurably contaminated with a 'totalitarian inclination' and operating through coercion. Vladimir Voinovich, Orwell's follower and himself a brilliant satirist and acute critic of the Soviet variety of totalitarianism, imagined the victory of the communist project (known to promise to allocate goods to everybody according to their needs) as a society in which each day starts with a governmental announcement of what today's needs of everybody are. . . It was not a society that questions its way of life that Orwell condemned, but a society in which some people, using their coercive powers, undertake to force some other people to change their way of life without so much as asking those other people's opinion.

There is all the difference, indeed the starkest of conceivable oppositions, between critically scrutinizing our own life practices, and forcing on others life practices not of their choice. The first is a condition *sine qua non* of human freedom; the other is a manifestation of human unfreedom. Orwell fulminated against a society tarnished with a totalitarian streak; a society up in arms against human freedom of choice. The purpose of sociology, I propose, is the expansion of human choice.

Cornelius Castoriadis, that passionate champion of genuine democracy, insisted that what is wrong with our society and what holds it away from true democracy is that it has ceased to question itself. I fully endorse his view.

How to do sociology?

Third: If there is a devaluation of values, men and women might come to feel either confused or humiliated: 'I used to value that. . .' It's one thing to devalue, but what can sociology offer instead? This is a question about why should men and women engage with sociology?

It is not a vocation or a task of sociology to impose value choices; moreover, it is not in sociology's power to do so even if it wished. The calling of sociology is to make value choice feasible and plausible, as well as bringing it closer into the reach of the individual burdened with the responsibility for finding proper solutions to socially generated life problems. To acquit itself of the demands of that calling, sociology needs to render the choices intelligible and the responsibilities involved evident. It is not a particular set of values that sociology is up against, but the assertion of TINA ('There Is No Alternative'), which, inspired by Margaret Thatcher, the present-day powers-that-be love to use and abuse. A choice is moral as long as it entails the acceptance of responsibility for its consequences – and first and foremost for its impact on the plight of others.

And this brings me to the 'confusion and humiliation' issue you've raised. You are right that laying bare and exposing the rather unprepossessing strings attached to the conduct practised thus far and believed to be flawless (as well as morally right) may and all too often does cause humiliation (a long-lasting pain and indelible stigma, unlike the 'confusion' which should be only a temporary condition shortly to be redeemed by recovered and renewed clarity). Fear of humiliation is a fertile soil for grassroots fundamentalisms and top-down totalitarianisms: those two desperate attempts to break communication, to shut the doors and slam the shutters in order to pre-empt the very possibility of exposure to otherness and preclude the very chance of any temptation to reconsider the ratio and the substance of self-identity. Or, even when it stops short of the extremes of fundamentalism or totalitarianism, fear of humiliation results in downgrading *Begegnungen* to the status of *Vergegnungen* (Martin Buber's terms) – encounters with others to 'mismeetings', quasi-meetings in which the protagonists do not really meet because they keep their ears clogged with stereotypes and prejudices and reduce contact to an exchange of blows, slanders and imputations. The human, all-too-human horror of being humiliated is indeed a major obstacle to all and any conversation worthy of its name – and also to that 'informal' (no procedural rules set in advance), 'open' (allowing the possibility of being found wrong) 'cooperation' (rather than a mere debate: no winners or losers here – everyone emerges from the exercise enriched in wisdom) whose model has been recently sketched by Richard Sennett and by which sociology should in my view measure the quality of its own encounters with its partners in conversation.

And so: how can I respond to your doubts? In only one way: yes, you are right, causing the feeling of humiliation is cruel; this is one cruelty which sociology has to risk, however, if it wants to remain faithful to its calling and social responsibilities. It should nevertheless do whatever is possible to mitigate, and better still to avoid that cruelty – and Sennett's model gives a clue as to how this can, hopefully, be done.

How to do sociology?

In your book Collateral Damage *(2011) you provide a short and insightful history of sociology and the discipline's perpetual quest for a scientific foundation and legitimacy. You also critically describe how sociology – or at least parts of the discipline – throughout its history has been bent on a managerial or technological mentality and an incurable data fetish), an objectification of the social world and its human members. Instead you opt for an alternative vision of sociology that privileges communication, the human subject, moral responsibility, critique and dialogue. How do you see the prospects of such a vision of sociology surviving and thriving in an academic world increasingly – at least in my view – characterized by and subjected to a logic of quantity, evidence and commercial or managerial utility of sociological knowledge? In other words, if sociology is – or perhaps rather should be – an ongoing critical dialogue with human life experience, as you have insisted, or 'an art of dialogue', how may this dialogue commence in a world, perhaps more than ever before, oblivious to, negligent of or perhaps even hostile to sociological wisdom?*

Oblivious to? Perhaps, and not unexpectedly; ours is, after all, a culture of surfing and forgetting. Negligent of? Perhaps as well, and again not unexpectedly; we bend and sag, after all, under the unbearable burden of excessive information, giving us little chance to slow down, reflect, and to separate the grain from the chaff. But hostile? On that charge, an unqualified verdict is ill-advised. I spy symptoms of hospitality alongside those of hostility; even of a strong and rising demand, albeit short on self-articulation and shamefully slow in breaking out of its confinement in the dungeons of the subconscious. Indeed, hostility to something signals in most cases hospitality to something else.

You are right in your diagnosis of the academic setting, including a sociology uncritical of its precepts and prohibitions, a sociology still struggling to be of use to the 'viable business' remembered from yesterday: to be of service to the managers from before their recent revolution. That sociology feels no particular pressure to urgently 'follow the tracks of the changing world' – the statute books of universities provide a protective shield against such pressure. Owing to the established procedure of graduation, promotion, staff rotation, self-replenishment and self-reproduction codified by those statute books, that sociology may cling infinitely to its extant form and style, oblivious to the 'changing world' and to the dwindling and evaporating demand for the services that such a form and style are capable of rendering. And that also means staying oblivious to the rising demand for an altogether different kind of service, which sociology would be able to render provided it revised its presently prevailing form and style, made, as you lucidly put it, to the measure of 'a managerial or technological mentality and an incurable data fetish'. In our increasingly deregulated, privatized and individualized world, this service, badly needed but so far sparingly supplied, needs to be rendered with the task (allow me to reach once more for your spot-on diagnosis) of a thorough '*de*-objectification of the social world and its human members' in mind.

I can only repeat what I wrote on this issue in my 2011 book *Collateral Damage* on the collateral casualties of inequality, restating the ideas formulated in my little book *Towards a Critical Sociology* of 1976:

How to do sociology?

For more than half a century of its recent history, and because it was seeking to be of service to managerial reason, sociology struggled to establish itself as a *science/technology of unfreedom*: as a design workshop for the social settings meant to resolve in theory, but most importantly in practice, what Talcott Parsons memorably articulated as 'the Hobbesian question': how to induce/force/indoctrinate human beings, blessed/cursed with the ambiguous gift of free will, to be normatively guided and to follow routinely a manipulable, yet predictable course of action; or how to reconcile free will with a willingness to submit to other people's will, lifting thereby the tendency to 'voluntary servitude', noted/anticipated by Étienne de La Boétie at the threshold of the modern era, to the rank of the supreme principle of social organization. In short: how to make people *will* doing what do they *must* . . .

In our society, individualized by decree of fate aided and abetted by the second managerial revolution, sociology faces the exciting and exhilarating chance of turning, for a change, into a *science and technology of freedom*: of the ways and means through which the individuals by decree and *de jure* of these liquid modern times can be lifted to the rank of individuals *by choice* and *de facto*. Or to take a cue from Jeffrey Alexander's call to arms in *A Contemporary Introduction to Sociology* (2008): sociology's future, at least its immediate future, lies in an effort to reincarnate and to re-establish itself as *cultural politics in the service of human freedom*.

And how to accomplish such a passage, what strategy to follow? The strategy consists in engaging in an ongoing dialogue with *doxa* or 'actor's knowledge', while observing, I repeat, the precepts of informality,

openness and cooperation, the formula recently suggested by Richard Sennett in his essay on 'Humanism'
and its present meaning (in the *Hedgehog Review* of
summer 2011), which needs to be thoroughly absorbed
and firmly memorized. 'Informality' means the rules of
dialogue are not pre-designed; they emerge in the course
of the dialogue. 'Openness' means that no one enters
the dialogue certain of their own truth and seeing it as
their only task to convince the others (holders, *a priori*,
of wrong ideas). And 'cooperation' means that in that
dialogue all participants are simultaneously teachers
and learners, while there are neither winners nor losers.

The price to be collectively paid for neglecting, col-
lectively, that advice can be the (collective) irrelevance
of sociology.

Many of the most important and flamboyant writers in
the history of sociology have been fond of metaphors.
Just think of the writings of C. Wright Mills, Erving
Goffman or Robert Nisbet, to mention a few outstand-
ing examples. Metaphors have also played an important
role in your own work, it seems that metaphors are
ways with which to navigate in and organize a com-
plex and changing world of immense possibility. Is this
perhaps the reason why some sociologists – including
yourself – find metaphors so intriguing to work with?

Querelles about the legitimacy and cognitive utility of
metaphors is as old as their uses, and repeating all the
arguments raised pro and contra in their course would be
as much a waste of time as pretending to start the debate
from scratch would be inane. What I am going to say,
pressed by your question, would therefore sound banal to

every historian of social science and more generally of philology, while remaining unconvincing to the uninitiated.

Metaphors come into their own whenever it comes to Gregory Bateson's 'tertiary learning' situation: the need to reassemble an established conceptual network too dense or rare to capture novel phenomena in a new cognitive frame to make salient their otherwise unnoticeable traits (as was the case with C. Wright Mills, Erving Goffman or Robert Nisbet, whose names you list to signpost a much wider tendency). A familiar notion is then used to evoke a vision in which the phenomenon in question can be placed to intuit its features.

Please note that metaphors are not expedients or stratagems peculiar to a specific school or resorted to by people with peculiar 'literary' predilections. They are unavoidable links in a chain of thoughts or moments in the process of thinking. They represent one of two (and only two, it seems) ways in which names for newly noted phenomena can be composed (the other being the formation of new words free of vocabulary associations). A successful metaphor is one which loses its birthmarks in the flow of time and ceases to be perceived as metaphorical. Few people except archivists are nowadays aware that the essential concepts of sociology entered its language, not such a long time ago, as metaphors (power, class, individual, group, human relations, social bonds – even 'society' itself, introduced in order to promote a then bold idea that the bizarre, newly developed and spotted or postulated 'imagined totalities' shared their features with all too familiar face-to-face company).

Your work is clearly characterized by an unmistakable 'essayistic edge' – you frequently, and some would say even frivolously, utilize literary insights and literary means such as metaphors, references to classic and contemporary literature and literary allusions in order to practise and present sociology. Why do you find it important or necessary to resort to these rather unconventional techniques when describing and analysing the human condition?

Were they still around and stooped to read my writings, the ancient sages would be among those 'some' inclined to call my use of metaphors frivolous. They (Plato most famously) held metaphors in rather low esteem, exiling them from the realm of the pursuit of truth and relegating them to the 'catch what you can' territory of rhetoric – even though they were anything but averse to lavishly availing themselves of metaphors' formidable cognitive capacity!

One uses metaphors, the ancients believed, as mere adornments of speech; as trinkets one would rather do without for the sake of clarity. Just as the Bauhaus people and other zealous modernists wished to cleanse buildings of all and any non-functional detail, they would cleanse all reasoning and arguments of metaphors. The sole purpose metaphors might serve, they insisted, was for the speaker to entreat and charm the listeners, to gain their applause and obtain approval prompted by whipped-up emotions instead of being solidly founded in alerted and watchful reason.

This is not, however, what metaphors do; or at least not the only task they can perform. In the case of an unfamiliar experience which needs an adequate conceptual net to catch and examine it, metaphors render an enormously important service. They serve imagination and comprehension. They are the indispensable scaffoldings for imagination and perhaps the most effective tools of comprehension.

Let's recall again, for example, that the core concept of sociology, the concept of 'society', was introduced into the emergent social-scientific discourse as a metaphor. Previously almost synonymous with 'company', evoking 'companionship', 'fellowship', 'association with one's fellow people in a friendly and intimate manner', the term 'society' was applied to an abstract totality anything but 'intimate' and not necessarily 'friendly' – and all that in order to grasp and visualize the invisible and intangible roots of the new and unfamiliar, yet unnamed pressures and dependencies of people, and to mentally map lines of dependency too extended and too far-reaching to be experienced 'at first hand' and subjected to direct sensuous scrutiny. Through the deployment of the metaphor of 'society', it was suggested that the unfamiliar condition could be absorbed into a familiar cognitive frame, that it was less alien or strange than otherwise would have been deemed, and that the already learned and tried forms of action could still be deployed to good effect. That operation was instrumental in recasting an aggregation inaccessible to the senses, an abstract totality of the 'population within a nation-state', into an 'imagined *community*'. It also had a performative ('perlocutionary', as John Austin would say) function: it chimed well with the struggle of the nascent modern state in the era of the 'primitive accumulation of legitimacy' to capitalize on the nostalgia its population displayed for the 'lost community'. The very fact that by now the metaphorical origins of 'society' have been largely forgotten and 'society' no longer feels like a metaphor when it is applied to the large, anonymous aggregate of state subjects testifies to the success of that operation.

Metaphorical juxtaposition also has another effect – largely unintended, though not necessarily for that reason cognitively useless, let alone harmful. On both sides of the juxtaposition, many a feature of the juxtaposed objects is left out of sight: a *similarity* is suggested, not *identity* – and in the case of similarity, differences are not denied, only bypassed and, so to speak, 'relegated to a lower league'. Metaphor simultaneously takes *pars pro toto* and *totum pro parte* – transforming the shapes of both invoked realms: noting and exposing existing similarities as much as conjuring up a new 'third' object. Metaphorical juxtaposition is an act of privileging and discriminating: some features are drawn into the limelight, some others cast into shadow ('bracketed away'). While the first kind of trait is assigned prime importance, the other traits are obliquely given less relevance – and attention is obliquely directed to or explicitly focused on the first. That kind of trait is suggested to 'play first fiddle', to 'set the tune', even to determine the rest of the object's traits. In all cases, the metaphor 'prejudices' the perception of the object it tries to comprehend.

Each metaphor is for that reason 'reductionist' – partial or even partisan. This is however, I believe, an inalienable feature of *all* cognition. The metaphor's claim to distinction derives solely from rendering that universal feature *easier to spot*; it is an irony, or the bad luck of metaphors that they tend to be reprimanded and denigrated for what could and should be counted among their great assets, rather than liabilities. Metaphors draw into the light the sorry lack of an 'overlap', indeed an ineradicable disparity, between words and 'things', knowledge and its object – as well as the inevitably 'construed' nature of objects: that limitation of all cognition that, once spotted, turns into a most effective stimulus to further cognitive effort, but could otherwise stay undetected, to the detriment, not the benefit, of knowledge (remember, for instance, Thomas S. Kuhn's 'anomaly' triggering scientific revolutions). Cognitive efforts, the intellectual assimilation and recycling of changing experience, the articulation of properly revised modes of life find powerful fertilizers in the 'leftovers' of metaphorical juxtapositions, while the hazy area surrounding the spotlighted bits is a most fertile ground for investigative action.

For the kind of sociology which I've chosen and try hard (even if not necessarily successfully) to practise – a sociology addressed to the actors of life dramas rather than to their scriptwriters, directors, producers and stage managers, a sociology moved by the urge to participate in the ongoing interpretation of their experience and of the strategies they construct and deploy in response, a sociology aimed at enhancing the scope of the actors' choices and assisting them in making the choices both reasonable and effective – such 'hazy areas' are a natural habitat and so metaphors are among principal tools: metaphors have the crucial advantage of opening up new sights while simultaneously exposing their limitations, their incurable non-comprehensiveness and non-finality.

Having noted the profusion of vibrating, unclear contours and blurred borderlines in Rembrandt's paintings, Georg Simmel (in his *Rembrandt: An Essay in the*

Philosophy of Art) praised those apparent violations of painting standards as manifestations of the painter's desire to grasp the true individuality of his (human!) objects which can never be reached through piling up crisply reproduced 'distinctive features' that, unlike human individuality, are as a rule common to many human beings and so hardly ever unique. Descriptions of human experience fail to meet (indeed, tend to be chronically and incurably incapable of meeting) the scientific standards of *Eindeutigkeit*, of clarity. But then humans are not ideal objects for scientific treatment, which humans invented in order to tackle, overpower, conquer and master non-human reality while preserving the immunity of their own freedom from its bonds and so our – human – freedom to act.

Yet another of Simmel's precepts addressed to the arts (this time from 'Der Fragment-charakter des Lebens' – 'the fragmentary character of life') is, I believe, applicable to sociology in equal measure. If it is true, says Simmel, that by their nature the arts aim at composing a complete, exhaustive and all-embracing universe, it is also true that every historically given form of art is only able to attain that purpose in part: no historically finite set of artistic forms will ever embrace the totality of the world's contents (that is, let me add, they will never grasp, lock up and seal the infinity of possibilities which human worlds carry or bring into being). Metaphors are good for thinking because they lay bare this dialectics of intention and performance and are not frightened by what they expose while doing it.

In many of your books, particularly from the 1980s and onwards, you have developed and deployed numerous

*metaphors – of different types of society ('solid modern',
'liquid modern'), of human beings and their stratified
experience of being in the world ('vagabonds', 'tour-
ists'), of different types of intellectuals ('legislators',
'interpreters') and of utopia ('gamekeeping', 'garden-
ing', 'hunting'), just to mention a few. What do you
expect from using these metaphors; what are the analytical promises and scientific merits, or lack of such, in
metaphors, as you see and utilize them?*

In her 'Metaphorical roots of conceptual growth' (in Lyn
D. English's edited *Mathematical Reasoning: Analogies,
Metaphors, and Images* 1997), Anna Sfard, a professor of mathematical education, quotes Carol Shields's
somewhat (though not entirely) humorous short story
under the tell-all title of 'The Metaphor is dead – pass
it on'. In Shields's story, a literature professor gives a
long speech against the use of metaphors, talks about
the effort to clean literature of any trace of them, and
then concludes: 'But alas, these newly resurrected texts
. . . still carry the faulty chromosome . . . of metaphor
since language itself is but a metaphorical expression of
human experience.' Sfard also quotes the groundbreak-
ing paper 'Metaphor' of 1955, in which Max Black
argued that in no way could 'the simple *comparison
view of metaphor* . . . account for our understanding of
this particular linguistic construction', and comments
that Black's 'main claim was that it is highly unlikely
that the basis for our use of one concept as a metaphor
for another is some simple similarity between these
two concepts. Similarity is *created* in the mind of the
conceivers of the metaphor rather than being *given* to
them, he posited. According to his *interaction* theory of

metaphor, our understanding of the metaphor's component concepts changes as a result of metaphorical projection.' And she concludes:

> Language is as much a part of concept-making as sounds are a part of making music. Rather than being viewed as a mere instrument for capturing ready-made ideas, it is ... the medium within which the creation of new concepts takes place. It is a bearer of conceptual structures we use to organize our experience. We have no other means for making sense of the world than what Lakoff and Johnson call image (or embodied) schemes – those language-dependent (although non-propositional in character), structure-imposing constructs which we carry through language from one context to another, whether we want it or not. Thanks to the transplants of conceptual structures, language itself is in a process of constant development. Like a living organism, it has the inevitability of change and growth inscribed in its genes. To sum up, one of the most important messages of the contemporary research on metaphors is that language, perception, and knowledge are inextricably intertwined.

Sorry for the lengthy quotation. I just could not deny myself the pleasure – she is after all my daughter, and it is a great joy to find that she can articulate ideas that I fully share much better than I would manage. And what Anna Sfard has articulated (and made indisputable, if only close attention is paid to her reasoning) is that thinking with the help of metaphors is not an activity for which one should feel obliged to apologize – unless one needs to apologize for being human, alive and living among humans.

The desperate efforts of many a scientist to cut off

all metaphorical roots and hide all traces of kinship with 'ordinary' (read: non-scientific, inferior to scientific) perception and thought are (perhaps an inevitable and certainly to be expected) part of a more general tendency of science, all too evident since Plato commanded philosophers to venture out of the cave, to put a distance between philosophy and the 'common sense' of the hoi polloi. (Gaston Bachelard famously dated the birth of modern science by the appearance of the first books that did not start from a reference to a common experience available to all.)

Scientists were successful in this respect, though only in part. Some sciences, having fenced off for themselves, or designed from scratch, a realm of 'empirical data' inaccessible to non-insiders (that is, to the rest of humanity), can also design a language similarly free of all semantic bonds with ordinary life and ordinary experience, being composed instead of custom-made terms with no past and no lateral associations. In the case of such sciences the postulate of banishing metaphors is perhaps plausible and feasible; it is also pragmatically useful, as it offers the additional benefit of underscoring and reinforcing the exile of common sense and its common carriers. Let us note, however, that as the sciences' independence from common experience has acquired material, fleshy, technically armed, imperturbable and unassailable foundations, that no longer need active defence by a discursive superstructure to be secure, the crusade against 'selective/reductionist' and somewhat 'imprecise' metaphors has lost much of its vigour and is fast running out of steam. Voices that some decades ago would have been condemned as heretical are now sounding out ever louder.

One of the most recent examples of such voices should suffice: S. Phineas Upham's article 'Is economics scientific? Is science scientific?' (in *Critical Review* in 2005). It develops Nancy Cartright's description of nature as 'tending to a wild profusion' and follows her call to 'construct different (scientific) models for different (cognitive) purposes' (exactly what metaphors do!) as 'no single model serves all purposes best'. Rightly, Upham suggests that if in the case of the 'natural sciences' (fortified, let me repeat, in a secure shelter of experience inaccessible and forever unfamiliar to 'ordinary folk') 'such an idea may be still viewed as a partisan, contentious standpoint, it is surely the sole and incontestable choice for the study of humans – as the behaviour of human beings is a domain that is too large, too complicated, and too unpredictable for any model to predict. . . This is why *different models* have *different functions*, and why *no one model can perfectly correspond to all permutations of the reality of human behaviour*' (emphasis added).

But this is precisely what metaphors do – consciously and openly. This is why they obey more faithfully than their detractors the injunction to be 'better mindful of the provisional nature of models, and scorn any tendency to sanctify laws derived from even the most pleasing or useful models'.

I admit that in using metaphors we set ourselves somewhat less ambitious, less pedantic or perfectionist goals than modern sciences did in the *Sturm und Drang* phase of their independence wars (and than the early social sciences did when they struggled to be admitted into their company). But I deny that this means that using metaphors is a sign of a lesser and inferior knowledge. Using metaphors derives from and signals our responsibility towards the prospective human objects/participants of the activity known under the name of 'sociology' – an activity that is the sole source of whatever authority we may claim and acquire. It signals a refusal to act under false pretences, to bid for greater authority than can realistically be claimed, or above all to distort the subject–object communication (yes, communication, since both the subject and the object are human and both have tongues) in favour of the subject (that is, the sociologist). This is not only a matter of choosing a cognitive strategy; it is also (and still more importantly) an *ethical* choice, a decision to assume responsibility for the voluntary or involuntary, subjective or objective responsibility of sociologists, and an act of assuming a moral stance towards the vocation and its prospective beneficiaries.

Siegfried Kracauer in *History: The Last Things before the Last*, points out that as 'parochial security' gives way to 'cosmopolitan confusion', there is a 'widespread feeling of powerlessness and abandonment', of 'being lost in uncharted and inimical expanses', which – dangerously – 'stirs many, presumably the majority of people, to scramble for the shelter of a unifying and comforting belief'. He then proceeds to praise Erasmus for being 'possessed with fear of all that is definitely fixed', since he believed that 'truth ceases to be true as soon as it becomes a dogma'. Knowing that 'none of the contending causes is the last word on the last issues at stake', one needs, as Kracauer insists, to seek 'a way of thinking and living which, if we could only follow it, would permit us to burn through the causes and thus to dispose of them – a way which for the lack of a better word, or a word at all, may be called humane'.

How to do sociology?

Well, such observations, much as their topicality must strike the twenty-first century reader, do not mean that the benefits of thinking with metaphors necessarily follow. . . Or do they?

You proposed the metaphor of 'liquid modernity' to capture the contemporary state of affairs. Looking through your recent work, you still stick to this metaphor. Moreover, several scholars working within a variety of disciplines – law studies, criminology, leisure studies, sociology, anthropology, social work, sports studies, religious studies, etc. – have now adopted it as an analytical framework for their own writings. Why has it proven to be so useful in describing, analysing and diagnosing contemporary society? And are you surprised by the sheer utility and indeed versatility of the notion of 'liquid modernity'?

When more than ten years ago I tried to unpack the meaning of the metaphor of 'liquidity' in its application to the currently practised form of life, one of the mysteries haunting me that obtrusively and staunchly resisted resolution was the status of the liquid modern human condition: is it an intimation, an early version, or an augury or portent of things to come? Or, rather, is it a temporary and transient as well as unfinished, incomplete and inconsistent interim settlement; an interval between two distinct, yet viable and durable, complete and consistent answers to the challenges of human togetherness?

I have not so far come anywhere near a resolution of that quandary, but I am increasingly inclined to surmise that – as you, Keith, have already insightfully noted following Antonio Gramsci's hint – we find ourselves at present in a time of 'interregnum': a state in which the old ways of doing things no longer work and the old learned and inherited modes of life are no longer suitable to the present-day *conditio humana*, but the new ways of tackling the challenges and the new modes of life more suitable for the new conditions have not as yet been invented, put in place and set in motion. We don't know yet which of the extant forms and settings will need to be 'liquidized' and replaced, though none seems to be immune to criticism and every one or almost every one has been earmarked for replacement at one time or another.

Most importantly, unlike our ancestors, we don't have a clear image of a 'destination' towards which we seem to be moving – which needs to be a model of *global* society, a global economy, global politics, global jurisdiction. Instead, we are reacting to the latest trouble, experimenting, groping in the dark. We try to diminish carbon dioxide pollution by dismantling coal-fed power plants and replacing them with nuclear plants, only to conjure up the spectre of Chernobyl and Fukushima to hover above us. We feel, rather than know (and many of us refuse to acknowledge), that power (that is, the ability to do things) has been separated from politics (that is, the ability to decide which things need to be done and given priority), and so in addition to our confusion about 'what to do' we are now in the dark about 'who is going to do it'. The sole agencies of collective purposive action bequeathed to us by our parents and grandparents, confined as they are to the boundaries of nation-states, are clearly inadequate, considering the global reach of our problems, of their sources and consequences.

We remain of course as modern as we were before

and certainly no less than any of our ancestors; but those 'we' who are modern have considerably grown in numbers in recent years. We may well say that by now all or almost all of us, in every or almost every part of the planet, are modern . . . And that means that today, unlike a decade or two ago, every land on the planet with only a few exceptions is subject to the obsessive, compulsive, unstoppable change now called 'modernization' and everything that goes with it, including the continuous production of human redundancy and of the social tensions it is bound to cause.

Forms of modern life may differ in quite a few respects – but what unites them all is precisely their fragility, temporariness, vulnerability and inclination to constant change. To 'be modern' means to modernize – compulsively, obsessively; not so much 'being', let alone keeping its identity intact, but forever 'becoming', avoiding completion, staying underdefined. Each new structure which replaces the previous one that was declared old-fashioned and past its use-by date is just another momentary settlement – regarded as temporary and 'until further notice'. Being always, at any stage and at all times, 'post-something' is also an undetachable feature of modernity. As time flows, 'modernity' changes its forms in the manner of the legendary Proteus. What was (erroneously) dubbed 'postmodernity' some time ago, and what I've chosen to call, more to the point, 'liquid modernity', is the growing conviction that change is *the only* permanence, and uncertainty *the only* certainty. A hundred years ago 'to be modern' meant to pursue 'the final state of perfection' – now it means an infinity of improvement, with no 'final state' in sight and none desired.

I did not think, before or now, of the solidity versus liquidity conundrum as a dichotomy; I view those two conditions as a couple inseparably locked in a dialectical bond (the kind of bond which François Lyotard probably had in mind when he observed that one can't be truly modern without being postmodern first). After all, it was the quest for the solidity of things and states that usually triggered, kept in motion and guided their liquefaction; liquidity was not an adversary but an effect of that quest for solidity, having no other parenthood, even though (or if) the parent would deny the legitimacy of the offspring. In turn, it was the formlessness of the oozing, leaking and flowing liquid that prompted the efforts of cooling, damping, casting and moulding. If there is something allowing for a distinction between the 'solid' and 'liquid' phases of modernity (that is, for them to be arranged in an order of succession), it is the change in both the manifest and the latent purpose behind the effort.

The original cause of melting solids was not the resentment felt for solidity as such, but dissatisfaction with the degree of solidity of the extant and inherited solids: purely and simply, the bequeathed solids were found not to be solid enough, to be insufficiently resistant and immunized to change by the standards of the order-obsessed and compulsively order-building modern powers. Subsequently however (and in our part of the world to this day), solids came to be viewed as evidently transient condensations of liquid magma; temporary settlements, rather than ultimate solutions. Flexibility has replaced solidity as the ideal condition of things and of affairs to be pursued. All solids (including those that may be momentarily desirable) are tolerated only in as far as they promise to remain easily and obe-diently fusible on demand. An adequate technology of melting must already be in hand even before the effort is started of putting together a durable structure, firm-ing it up and solidifying it. A reliable assurance of the right and ability to dismantle the constructed structure must be offered before the job of construction starts in earnest. Fully 'biodegradable' structures – starting to disintegrate the moment they have been assembled – are nowadays the ideal and the standard to which most, if not all structures struggle to measure up.

To cut a long story short, if in its 'solid' phase the heart of modernity was in controlling and fixing the future, in the 'liquid' phase the prime concern moved to the avoidance of mortgaging it and of any other threat that might pre-empt exploitation of the still undisclosed, unknown and unknowable opportunities which the future is hoped and bound to bring. Friedrich Nietzsche's spokesman Zarathustra, in anticipation of such a human condition, bewailed 'the loitering of the present moment' that threatens to make the Will, burdened with the thick and heavy deposits of its past accomplishments and misdeeds, 'gnash its teeth', groan and sag, crushed by their weight. Fear of things that are fixed too firmly to permit dismantling, things over-staying their welcome, things tying one's hands and shackling one's legs, the fear of following Faustus to hell after having committed, as he did, the blunder of wishing to arrest a beautiful moment and to make it stay forever – this fear was traced back by Jean-Paul Sartre to our visceral, extemporal and inborn resentment of touching slimy or viscous substances; yet, symptomati-cally, that fear was only pinpointed as a prime mover of human history at the threshold of the liquid modern era. That fear, in fact, signalled the imminent arrival of modernity. And we may view its appearance as a fully and truly paradigmatic watershed in history.

Of course, as I've stated so many times, the whole of modernity stands out from preceding epochs by its compulsive and obsessive modernizing – and modernizing means liquefaction, melting and smelting. But – but! Initially, the major preoccupation of the modern mind was not so much the technology of smelting (most of the apparently solid structures around melted seemingly out of their own incapacity to hold up) as the design of the moulds into which the molten metal was to be poured and the technology of keeping it there. The modern mind was after perfection – and the state of perfection it was hoped would be reached meant in the last account the end to strain and hard work, as all further change could only be a change for the worse. Initially, change was viewed as a preliminary and interim measure which it was hoped would lead into an age of stability and tranquillity – and so also to comfort and leisure; it was seen as a necessity confined to the time of transition from the old, rusty, partly rotten, crumbling and fissiparous, and otherwise unreliable and altogether inferior structures, frames and arrangements, to their made-to-order, ultimate because perfect, replacements: windproof, waterproof, and indeed history proof. Change was, so to speak, a movement towards the splendid vision at the horizon: a vision of an order, or (to recall Talcott Parsons's crowning synthesis of modern pursuits) of a 'self-equilibrating system' able to emerge victorious from every imaginable disturbance and stubbornly and irrevocably returning back to its state: an order resulting from a thorough and irrevocable 'skewing of probabilities' (maximizing the probability of some events, minimizing the likelihood of others). Just like accidents, contingency, melting pots, ambiguity, ambivalence, fluidity and other banes and nightmares of the order-builders, change was seen (and tackled) as a *temporary irritant* – and most certainly not undertaken for its own sake (it is the other way round nowadays: as Richard Sennett has observed, perfectly viable organizations are now gutted just to prove their ongoing viability).

Your analysis, or perhaps rather diagnosis, of contemporary liquid modernity is reminiscent in many obvious ways of the work of Karl Marx and Friedrich Engels and their incisive depiction of how 'all that is solid melts into air', just as it reminds one of Max Weber's insightful and gloomy idea of the 'iron-cage of rationality' and the concomitant 'disenchantment of the world'. Once you wrote – commenting on how sociologists interpret and describe the human world they study – that 'we do not live, after all, once in a pre-modern, once in a modern, once in a postmodern world. All three "worlds" are but abstract idealizations of mutually incoherent aspects of the single life-process which we all try our best to make as coherent as we can manage' (from Mortality, Immortality and Other Life Strategies, *1992). Although 'liquid modernity' is perhaps just yet another intellectual label intended to capture the complexities of contemporary society, an academic abstraction meant to give shape to a persistently shapeless world, it nevertheless makes one wonder what comes next in real life as well as in intellectual attempts to idealize it. In short, what awaits us at the end of liquid modernity? Knowing*

that you insist – and rightly so – that you have no abili-
ties to look into the future or predict what waits around
the next corner, have you given this any thought and
consideration?

The fact that having explored in relative depth and full-
ness the way we live under liquid modern conditions,
as well as the fashions in which we, sociologists, try
to grasp that mode of life and restructure our subject-
matter in order to assist our fellow humans in facing
up to the challenges with which such a way of life confronts them, we are no wiser now than we were at the
beginning of our conversation as to the destination of
the ongoing and far from finished human adventure –
that itself is perhaps the best answer to your question;
it certainly is the sole answer I am able to articulate and
responsibly offer.

Ours, I repeat after Keith, is a period of 'interregnum': of a time in which old ways of doing things
daily manifest their inadequacy, whereas the new and
more effective ways hoped to replace them have not yet
reached the planning stage. This is a time when anything
or almost anything can happen – but little if anything
can be undertaken with certainty, or at least a fairly
large probability of success. I suspect that predicting
the destination towards which we are moving under
such conditions (and even less a destination at which
we are bound to arrive in as a result) is irresponsible
and misleading, since the impossibility of a purposeful
action which would reach the roots of liquid modern
problems, and the absence of agencies able to undertake
it and see it through, is precisely what defines those
conditions.

This does not mean that we should stop trying – but it does mean that while never ceasing to try we need to treat every successive attempt as an interim settlement, one more experiment in need of thorough testing before it is proclaimed a 'destination' or a 'solution' to our quandaries.

Sociology has always been tied to the word – books, articles, lectures. But ours is a culture ever increasingly dominated by the visual. What implications does this have for how sociology is practised? Should sociology remain tied to the word and thus offer an alternative to the visual, or should it try to engage in conversation in ways closest to those of contemporary culture?

Yes, the younger generations of the human race grow up in a world ever more packed with images and ever less with words (which also tend to get shorter and all too often monosyllabic and vowel-free). And yes, sociology because of its hermeneutic tasks is bound to remain, as are all hermeneutics, 'tied', as you say, 'to the word' (not a bad thing in itself, as words help the individual psyche to develop its imaginative skills, which images on the whole reduce or render redundant altogether). But then there are words and there are words . . . *succulent* (one could say 'sensual') words that appeal to the listener's imaginative powers and evoke and rouse images, and *desiccated* words, born and dying in the universe of abstract concepts – to that universe, images are not invited due to their emotive capacities and affinities and they would be chased from it were they to try to enter.

Georg Christoph Lichtenberg, whose acute and astute aphorisms accompanied the birth pangs of the modern mind, anticipated the predicament long before images started flooding the human world and drowning out human speech: 'A sensation expressed in words is like music described in words; the expressions we use are not sufficiently one with the thing to be expressed. The poet who wants to excite sympathy directs the reader to a painting, and through this to the thing to be expressed. A painted landscape gives instant delight, but one celebrated in verse has first to be painted in the reader's own head . . .'

If we agree that sociology finds itself in today's liquid modern society in an entirely different landscape than in its early years of inception and formation, one may wonder: what is sociology's audience today – and has it changed with the transformation from what you term 'solid' to 'liquid' modernity? Who listens and learns from sociologists these days? And in contemporary culture has the mode of listening also changed? For example, students today seem less interested in reading books, but they eagerly scan web pages and listen to lots of podcasts, earplugs firmly cutting them off from the outside world. Where does this leave sociology?

Sociology spent the first part of its history trying to be of service to the modern project and obsession of order building: it defined its task as designing social arrangements fit to answer what Talcott Parsons, the codifier and the major apostle of that faith, called 'the Hobbesian question': how to induce, force or indoctrinate human beings, blessed and cursed as they are with the ambiguous and endemically prankish gift of free will, to be normatively guided – and to routinely follow an orderly, predictable course of action; how to make people to do *voluntarily* and *gladly* what they *must* and/ or are *compelled* to do. Sociology was then, so to speak, a 'science and technology of unfreedom'.

In our increasingly individualized liquid modern society, in which the resolution of socially created problems is relentlessly shifted from social powers on to the shoulders of individual men and women, however, sociology has the chance (though, admittedly, no more than that!) to turn instead into a *science and technology of freedom*: that is, knowledge of the ways and means by which the individuals *by decree* and *de jure* of liquid modern times can be lifted to the rank of individuals *by choice* and *de facto*. This is, as I endlessly repeat, a *chance* – though I believe that it is also, and even in the first place, a *moral obligation*: the task which sociology owes to the men and women of our times. But to acquit itself honourably of this moral duty, sociology needs to engage nowadays in a *continuous dialogue with the daily experience of those men and women*.

I'd say that the twin roles which we, sociologists, are called on to perform in that dialogue are those of *defamiliarizing the familiar* (debunking its alleged self-evidence) and *familiarizing* (taming, domesticating, making manageable) *the unfamiliar*. Both roles demand skills in uncovering and clarifying the influences and dependencies that humans need to cope with whenever they confront the tasks they are forced and expected (counterfactually, in all too many cases) to perform individually, with individual resources and at their individual risk.

The kind of dialogue I have in mind is a difficult art. It involves committing the partners in conversation to an intention to *jointly* clarify the issues, rather than to win the argument and carry one's own point; to *multiply* voices, rather than to reduce their number; to *widen* the set of possible sequels, rather than denigrate and exclude all alternatives; and thereby to jointly pursue understanding, instead of aiming at defeating alternative views – and all in all to be animated by a wish to *keep the conversation going*, rather than by a desire *to grind it to a halt*. Mastering that art is terribly time-consuming, though far less time-intensive than practising it. It also calls for humility, surrendering the privileges of the unerring expert, exposing oneself to the risk of being proven wrong.

A 'risk of losing technical quality in an process' is an apprehension prominent among the 'difficulties' and 'obstructions' in such a shift. Once human beings, in addition to being objects of our study, also become our partners in dialogue, and in a dialogue calculated to service *their* needs and respond to *their* quandaries, sociologists lose the luxury enjoyed by the sciences of the non-human: the privilege of ignoring any opinions held by the objects of their study, and exercising full, indivisible and inalienable, 'professional' sovereignty over meaning creation and over the separation of truth from untruth. The 'technical' quality of the study then acquires a new sense; where dialogue is concerned, that quality is measured by the progress of *mutual* comprehension and by relevance to the interests and tasks of the *objects* of research, rather than to those of the researchers themselves. It is that loss (or rather voluntary surrender) of the monopoly on interpretive rights, and our agreement to share them with our 'objects', that is mistaken by some for the 'loss of technical quality'.

The ultimate purpose of the education in which sociologists would then engage (as the line separating communication in general, and dialogue in particular, from reciprocal education is anything but fixed, clear and non-negotiable) is preparation of our partners in conversation for life, and sociology of the kind I've practised is bent on preparing them for life in the kind of society in which our pupils or students are bound to live and which they themselves will be making while being made by it. Having already been sentenced to individuality, our students will still need to lift themselves from being individuals merely by decree of fate to being individuals *de facto*: able to assert themselves, to choose the kind of life they wish to lead, and to follow that choice. Sociology may help to make them aware of what this endeavour is likely or bound to involve, and so expand their options, and by the same token serve the cause of their freedom.

So the public for sociology is to be made by sociology? Does this mean that sociology is necessarily linked to a public, but not necessarily to a public demanded by the protagonists of social science?

Michael Burawoy alerted us all that sociology was losing its link to the public arena. Following his hint, I suggested then that an academic sociology groomed and honed to serve managerial reason was singularly unfit to properly service the emergence of a radically different public composed of individuals now burdened with functions abandoned and 'subsidiarized' in the course of the ongoing 'managerial revolution mark two'. I suggested that a thorough readjustment of sociology (of its agenda and problematics, strategic goals, language) is now, literally, a life-or-death matter for the discipline. What is called for is a change in its status and character from a science and technology of unfreedom to a science and technology of freedom. This is admittedly a highly demanding endeavour. But it is one which is capable of opening up to sociology an unprecedentedly vast public and an equally unprecedented public demand for its services.

Some of your recent books, especially from Postmodernity and Its Discontents (1997) *onwards, seem to entertain a certain element of nostalgia in that you appear to decry the state of the contemporary social scene. Would you agree with the claim that your books contain nostalgic undertones? Do you see any function of nostalgia in sociology?*

I know of no arrangement of human togetherness, present or past, which could be seen as an optimal solution to the aporia of the human condition. It seems that linearity of history, by whatever criterion it is plotted, could be a product only of reductionism (when reported) or a utopian stance (when projected). The trajectory of successive rearrangements is more reminiscent of a pendulum than a straight line. Each arrangement has tried to reconcile incompatible demands, but the efforts as a rule ended with resigning a part of one for the sake of gratifying a part of another. And so each rearrangement sooner or later inspired a demand for another; each next step brought more of the 'good things' which had gone missing – but at the expense of some other things whose 'goodness', indeed indispensability, was revealed only after the exchange was made (their 'goodness' stayed unnoticed as long as they were 'self-evident', or unproblematic to the point of invisibility). The other way to say the same thing is that each improvement brought new shortcomings (or re-evaluation of old). As Friedrich Wilhelm Schelling opined almost two centuries ago, *Erinnerung* (reminiscence) is a 'retrospective impact' of the end on the beginning; beginnings stay unclear until the end is reached, and the antecedents reveal themselves only through their consequences. We may add that the 'revelation' of the 'unclear' is not a one-off event, but in principle an infinite process, and that – contrary to its definition – 'the past' is as motile as its sequels, which go on reshuffling and reassessing its contents.

For many years now I've been repeating after Sigmund Freud that 'civilization' (meaning a social order) is a trade-off, in which some values are sacrificed for the sake of others (usually it is the lot of those values that seem to exist in sufficient quantity to be given away in order to attain more of the values that are felt to be in short supply). In these terms, one may say that the history of systemic changes is a succession of trade-offs.

The passage from the 'solid' to the 'liquid' variety of modern life was a reversal of the trade-off which Freud noted in the passage to modernity. The centuries that followed the disintegration of the *ancien régime* (the pre-modern order) could be described retrospectively as a long march towards restitution (on a different level and with different means) of the shattered security; we are now in the midst of another long march, this time towards dismantling the constraints imposed on individual liberties in the course of the long march to security which rested on intensive and extensive normative regulation and thorough policing. Let me note, though, that this new 'long march' seems to be destined to be much shorter than its predecessor. Signs gather, and quickly, of a return of old value preferences. Symptoms accumulate of a new tendency to trade off personal liberties for personal (corporeal, bodily?) safety. This new tendency is not a return to a preoccupation with the kind of securities described by Freud; rather, it signals another turn of the pendulum between security and freedom – solidity and flexibility, determination and open-endedness, constraint and uncertainty.

What you see as 'nostalgia' is perhaps a reflection of the unpleasant, though hardly avoidable fact that the full costs of a new trade-off can be calculated only at the end of the accounting period. For the 'leap to order' (as I tried to document in *Modernity and the Holocaust* and *Modernity and Ambivalence*) an enormous and atrocious price had to be paid – but this does not mean that repairing the unprepossessing features of 'solid' modernity ushered in a cloudless and faultless form of human togetherness that would leave no room for dissent. Each arrangement has, I repeat, its own shortcomings crying for attention – and each needs to be judged in terms of its own virtues and vices. And due to the 'pendulum-like' trajectory of historical sequences, a close proximity between 'forward and backward' or 'utopia' and 'nostalgia' that is pregnant with confusion is virtually inevitable.

Should the author control the meanings of his or her work once it has been published? What if the work is interpreted and construed in ways the author finds completely unacceptable, for instance politically or ethically? Is that just something we – sociologists as writers – must learn to live with?

There is nothing to stop her or him from trying, though I wouldn't predict much chance for full, or even partial yet satisfactory success. Deciding to go public involves making the text a hostage to (unknown and never fully predictable, let alone controllable) fate. Once sent, the messages carry their own, autonomous lives. In communication, the intended meaning of messages and their perceived meaning are linked, but the second is never totally determined by the first. I'd even say that in the ensuing controversy the author's version enjoys no superior authority over the recipients' readings, since the emergent meanings are as a rule the products of interaction between the text and the cognitive frames formed by the readers' variegated experiences.

You are right in adumbrating that 'sociologists as writers' 'must learn to live with' the prospect of losing control over the interpretation of their messages – though I'd insist that the duty of a responsible writer is to work hard on their skills of expression, reducing their ambiguity to a minimum; even if the total elimination of controversy is not on the cards because of the ineliminable ambiguity of living vernaculars. If indeed interpretations appear which 'the author finds completely unacceptable' in most cases the author has only their own negligence, laxity or slovenliness to blame.

4
What does sociology achieve?

MHJ and KT *What is the use of sociology?*

ZB I believe that sociology should be judged by its relevance to experience and humans' struggles with their own life problems, and not by loyalty to methodology. It's risky, very risky, full of traps and ambushes whenever we want to speak, not so much to illustrious colleagues, as to the ordinary people out there. All the same, they are the genuine recipients of our services. Either they are our genuine recipients, finding our services of importance, use and benefit to them, or there's no point in doing our job at all because the fear that sociology is losing touch with the public sphere will really be true. The relevance to common mundane experience is in my view the only link nowadays connecting us to 'the public sphere'.

Recently, an insightful (some might say whippersnapper) sociology undergraduate blatantly stated during an examination: 'The biggest challenge confronting

*sociology today is how to be taken seriously.' Do you
agree with this? Or are there other challenges to sociology that we need to be concerned about?*

Knowingly or not, your undergraduate compressed
two (or is it three?) questions into one. Two obvious
questions are (1) can sociological interpretations of
worldly things be taken seriously, and (2) can the things
sociology interprets be taken seriously? Yet there is, I
suspect, a third question underlying the first two and
prodding your undergraduate, and not just him, to ask
them: are we, the intended addressees and beneficiaries
of sociological interpretations, able or inclined to take
seriously the messages they convey? Of the three, only
the first question, embracing and presuming the other
two and doing it explicitly, addresses, as your gradu-
ate probably assumed, sociological craftsmanship and
implies the need to take a closer look at sociological
practice; to compose a list of its deficiencies and to propose, as well as apply, effective remedies. The second
question and particularly the third, however, inquire
into affairs well beyond the reach of the self-referential
preoccupations of the practitioners of sociological
craftsmanship and their self-criticizing, self-reforming
and self-healing capacities.

'Taking sociology seriously' is a challenge not essentially different from the charge to take seriously any
other kind of knowledge – to take it seriously on the
strength of the assumed expertise of its sources in a
world saturated with opinions vying with each other
and corroding each other's genuine or imputed veracity.
Not 'essentially' different, yet more difficult to handle
than in the case of many other academically institution-

alized sciences, and that, I suggest, for a reason which lies in the very nature of sociology as a dialogue with so-called 'common sense': the subject-matter of sociological investigation is shared with its objects. Sociologists and the (similarly human!) objects of their study tell stories about 'the same' experience, and there is no immediate reason to assign greater value to the stories told by the craftspeople of sociology – unlike in the case of stories told by physicists, geologists or astronomers, stories concerning objects and events placed well beyond the life experience of ordinary (uninitiated and un-accredited) men and women and so *a priori* escaping any non-professional test of their veracity. The line separating an accredited 'expert', a carrier of professional credentials, from a 'lay person' (a not-knower, not allowed to speak with authority) is much thinner in the case of sociology than in the case of many other disciplines, and an object of much greater contention, and much less likely ever to be resolved.

Not knowing any more about their objects of study than the objects do themselves is a potential obstacle to 'being taken seriously', and is specific to sociology as a profession. Less specific, if at all, is another challenge, however, boomeranging on the seriousness with which sociology is treated: the challenge of the subject-matter of their study being taken seriously. That other challenge derives from the all-too-evident unreliability (fluidity, inconsequentiality, contingency) of the part of reality under study. Life in a liquid modern setting teaches (or at least suggests or implies) the brevity of the life expectation of any message and any institution vouching for its authority at the moment of sending. The distance in time between heresy and superstition, between truths being proclaimed 'before their time' and being discredited as outdated or erroneously born, between the prescription for success and a recipe for failure, or between cutting-edge technology and the rubbish heap, is scarily brief and shows every sign of shortening further.

Learner, beware! Clutching tightly to the knowledge you've gained and habits you've acquired spells trouble to come. Irony, distance, non-commitment, and above all an awareness of the 'until further noticeness' of truths is one of those few pieces of advice of the current version of reason that should – indeed – be taken seriously. To no other field does this apply more than to the area of knowledge of 'the social', the part of reality known to excel and overtake all other areas in chameleon-like and kaleidoscopic change. The agony of social institutions starts the day after their birth. So does the agony of fashions, objects of public interest and popular cravings or fears, 'talks of the town' and 'the only games in town'. Signposts move faster than it takes to reach the destinations to which they point. With experience like this accumulating, it is a risky business to treat seriously any reports on the 'state of the world', let alone prognoses of its future states. For better or worse, our contemporaries are trained in the art of flexibility, liquid modernity's 'authoritatively endorsed and recommended', as well as popularly acclaimed meta-value . . .

Which brings me to the third question – thus far the least investigated and so the furthest as yet from a satisfactory answer. Are we not ever less capable of taking seriously not only the whirlwind of information, but the state of affairs itself which they claim to notify or warn us about, together with the responsibilities deriving from them? Are we not feeling overwhelmed by the flood of information and so 'secondarily *ignorant*' (not because of a deficit of knowledge, but due to its indigestible and unassimilable excess), but also *impotent* (meaning that we feel we wouldn't be able to avert the catastrophe even if we knew for sure that it was approaching)? Aren't we therefore, for those reasons, incapable of taking a firm stance, of insisting and persisting, and staying insistent and persistent for a sufficiently long duration – suspecting that whatever we do will have little effect and that long-term engagement would amount to a wasteful loss of resources and energy? Many of the factors we've discussed may contribute to this 'trained incapacity' – and the crisis of agency more than any other aspect of the present-day social reality. Sociology being in the frontline of the battle to grasp, record and comprehend that social reality and the role of human agency in its formation and reproduction may feel their effects stronger than other fields of scholarship. As so often and in all sorts of cases, the condemnation of the message rebounds on the messenger.

Sociology might have this potential of entering into a wide dialogue, but it's only some *sociology that does that, certain kinds of sociology, clearly yours more than, say, studies of drug abuse in certain areas of cities, statistics, and so forth. So sociology has this potential and yet the only sociologists seen as having the legitimacy to try to achieve that potential are those with professional status. Is there a paradox there? If you don't mind it being put this way, you've recently received a significant number of very prestigious prizes, and this gives you authority as an intellectual, as a sociologist. Does that authority which is attributed to you get in the way of your message getting out, get in the way of your work having any dialogue?*

No, this is not the question . . . The question is whether the people you address recognize their problems in what you are saying, whether the communication is really reciprocal and you are not a voice crying in the wilderness. No, if you are able to put the sociological problem in a way relevant to the predicament people feel they find themselves in but also find difficult to articulate and render intelligible. I still see no reason to rebel against the Enlightenment idea that acting with knowledge is more on a par with human freedom and autonomy, and so all in all better, than acting in a state of ignorance. What follows is that to supply the successive bits missing in deciphering and comprehending the conditions under which we act is a great job; as well as potentially a lot more than previous generations of sociologists managed to accomplish.

But to return for a moment to what we have already discussed: nothing here is predetermined, the two sharply different models of sociology can coexist for a long time to come. Describing scientific revolutions, Thomas S. Kuhn emphasized that the accumulation of knowledge is not smooth, occurring uniformly and synchronically in the whole scholarly discipline; reformations as a rule have their counterreformations, and the road to assimilation of new knowledge is rife with splits and divided loyalties as well as internecine warfare between orthodoxies and heresies. Periods of truce are likely to be short-lived, while efforts to disgrace, disempower, delegalize and eliminate the opposite camps become the rule.

I don't imply that there is just one strategy to be taken and one way in which sociology can be done. The continued advantage of the kind of sociology I am protesting against, the one I believe has indeed 'lost its link to the public arena', is that it offers to those who wish for it a way to join clear-cut 'career tracks', established trajectories leading to a doctorate, lectureship and chair. Once you've mastered the obligatory methodology of garnering and processing facts, it does not matter much how grave the issues you investigate in your dissertation and how great the social need and demand for your findings. The sole thing that truly matters for an average career is whether you departed from the methodology of your masters sitting on the examining committee, or and whether or not you are loyal. This is indeed what Abraham Maslow defined as a stratagem invented to serve non-creative people wishing to join the creative effort.

And so the future of academic sociology, even its short-term future, is in no way predetermined. There are quite powerful odds against a rush to embrace the new challenges and opportunities open to the sociological vocation: there are vested interests which have developed in keeping intact the inherited ways of doing sociology. And there will always be things hitherto uncounted and therefore offering the chance for another count. The might of institutionalized inertia may outweigh the pressure of new social circumstances. But it may also happen that sociology acquires a relevance far beyond the academic establishment and manages to reach people who really need these sorts of services.

What does sociology achieve?

Most of your work has been carried out on your own and without funding from research agencies. In this sense, you are equivalent to what Karl Mannheim once termed a 'free-floating intellectual' ...

I explain the pursuit of research funding (the more massive the better!) as a side-effect of the desperate attempt of sociologists, cast and fixed as they are in the academic setting, to create artificial means of keeping their distance from 'lay' or 'common' sense and to claim the superiority of the knowledge they themselves generate and endorse. It may also be useful in helping to find a demand for one's own work among the practitioners of what Foucault named 'demographic' rule. Apart from those two functions, funding is hardly a necessary condition of sound sociological investigation.

And I steer clear of collective (committee-style) undertakings. Hannah Arendt suggested that thinking is the most solitary of human activities, and from my personal experience I tend to endorse that impression. Yet I find as well that thinking is dialogical ... And yet most of the collective publications I have browsed through are anything but paragons of dialogue and manifestations of its creative powers.

You once said that when supervising and guiding a PhD student, although feeling ambivalent and internally divided, you would always make sure that the creativity and artistic aspirations of the thesis would not prevent it from passing the approval of the PhD committee. For up-and-coming sociologists, for the next generation of people practising the noble art and science of sociology, could you offer some tricks of the trade – not about how to create a career out of sociology, but about how to make sure of having something interesting and, not the least, important to say?

What can I say at the end of my own road? If you are after a comfortable life, look elsewhere. Obviously, doing sociology is not a recipe for getting rich, but neither is it a prescription for a trouble-free existence. It is, at the utmost (but I wouldn't underestimate, or in any way play down, the importance of that particular utmost!), a way to life fulfilment – to a gratification offered by work well done for the sake of leaving the world, the shared abode of human beings, in a condition just a little bit better (and above all not worse) than the one in which it was found on entry.

I doubt whether there is a set of rules to guarantee success that one can learn to avoid blunders and be certain of reaching the goal. The rulebook needs to be kept permanently open, with enough pages left blank to accommodate new rules – as they emerge, as they must, in the course of successive practices deployed in successive conditions. The world is changing and re-arranging itself (not without our cooperation, by design or default) much too fast for any set of rules to remain workable for the duration of an individual life, let alone to outlive it.

And so, rather than waste time on fortune-telling, let's go to work. And go on as long as our strength allows and our dedication to the task – that one constant and undying variable in the equation – dictates.

If we agree that sociology is, and should be, a critical engagement with the world of common sense and doxa, the world of the taken-for-granted, the naturalized world, the world apparently and stubbornly impervious to change and critique, of what use is critique – and with it sociology – then? Many years ago, in your book Towards a Critical Sociology *(1976) you proposed that such a critical engagement with the world might be seen as an emancipatory interest and that the emancipation of reason was a condition of all material emancipation. Do you still see it this way, and if so, how is this emancipation of man to be achieved?*

The concept of 'emancipation' suggests the removal of all or some of the constraints cramping and so narrowing the range of available options and realistic choices; in a nutshell, it implies 'more freedom'. The expression 'material emancipation' is therefore an oxymoron; it refers to the world, not to its perception; it belongs to the semantics of ontology, not epistemology. Your query is about the possibility and capacity for a change in *perception* to cause or at least to influence (render more or less probable) a change in the *world*. A question, as you know well, timeless in the history of philosophical worldviews – as timeless as the search for its answers. I would rather recall here the popular English wisdom of eating being the proof of the pudding. The elusiveness of whether the sought-after answer stands a sporting chance of universal – and durable – approval arises from the fact that it can be offered solely by *practice*, not *theorizing*. In philosophy, both the positive and the negative answers to that question muster enough persuasive arguments to erode the persuasiveness of their opposites. And as to the practice, no one has been more closely on target than Vaclav Havel, himself a consummate practitioner of the art of changing the world through ideas. To influence the future, he said, one needs to know what songs the nation is inclined to sing; but, he added right away, no one can tell what sort of songs the nation will be willing to intone next year. That verdict, with which Theodor W. Adorno would, I guess, wholeheartedly agree (as do I), wouldn't have stopped him from nudging, stirring and exhorting nations to change the tunes they intoned, to reform their current habits and inclinations; even though in moments of reflection he would have accepted the prospect of sealing his exhortations, and so his critique of the status quo, in a bottle left to the admittedly unpredictable vagaries of the tides . . .

Let me clarify the issue a bit further. The intimate link between reality and its perception (or perception and the reality which it generates and/or sustains) is not a postulate but an inseparable attribute of the human existential condition (if you prefer to use Heidegger's vocabulary, of the specifically human modality of being-in-the-world). The world we inhabit is the *Lebenswelt*, the 'lived world', and that entails ontology as much as epistemology, reality (what can't be 'wished away') and its perception (potentially possible to be argued away, by design or default). The issue in question therefore boils down to the feasibility, or likelihood, of causing shifts in perception – and through them prompting desirable changes in reality. In other words: *changing reality through changing its perception.*

Being fully aware of how much that issue has been and remains contentious, I don't entertain any hope (or for that matter ambition) to resolve the contention. I settle for a minimalist stance: being knowledgeable is better than being ignorant – and even if the presence of knowledge is not a guarantee of successful action, its absence most certainly tends to diminish the probability of an action's success. In particular, the chances that something will be attempted that is unprecedented and steps beyond the habitual routine grow once the objects of action are drawn out of invisibility and into the field vision and awareness; in Heideggerian terms, the chances of recasting fragments of reality into objects of purposeful action grow once those fragments are transferred from the status of *zuhanden* ('at hand', routinely graspable, 'hiding in their [dazzling, blinding] familiarity', so to speak) to that of *vorhanden* ('out there', stubborn and resistant, intriguing, calling for scrutiny, spurring to action). I believe that it is the vocation of sociology to draw the human world out of the invisibility of 'doxa' (common, unreflected-upon sense – knowledge we think *with*, but hardly ever *about*) to become the focus of attention, area of awareness and field of purposeful action – through defamiliarizing the familiar and problematizing the unproblematic. Rather than *postulating* sociology to be critical, I suppose that sociology loyal to its vocation *is* critical: willy-nilly, consciously or not, by the sheer logic of its enterprise.

I willingly admit the banality of these statements – and repeating them while conversing with you therefore makes me feel somewhat embarrassed. And yet one needs to restate them, since sociological routine all too often covers up their message and conceals the precepts that follow it out of our sight and 'proactive' attention. And that happens in spite the evidence of the tremendous difference made by the contents of the *Lebenswelt* to the inclinations, motivation and, all in all, the life strategies of the people who 'live it' (that is, who make it while being made by it). Just one off-the cuff example: though today we speak freely and matter-of-factly of, say, medieval or even Palaeolithic cultures (therefore taking for granted the contrived, arte factual, choice-based nature of the ways in which humans of all eras and places conduct their lives), the very concept of 'culture', and the tacit yet seminal assumptions it carries, were formed and brought into the public vocabulary and *doxa* only in the third quarter of the eighteenth century. It is obvious, or at least it ought to become obvious with a minimum of reflection, that the presence of the idea/vision of 'culture', with all its conceptual and pragmatic luggage, is one of those key, indeed watershed 'differences that make the difference' between modern and pre-modern modes of living-in-the-world. An even more striking illustration of the role as '*Lebenswelt*-building blocks' of the concepts people use when forming their perceptions and selecting their strategies is provided by the knowledge of mortality that sets apart the human mode of being-in-the-world from the modes practised by all other living species (animals, we can say, are immortal, because they do not know of their mortality, even though they are equipped with the instinctual tendency to avoid or stave off death). It may be said with good reason that culture, the defining trait of the uniquely human mode of being-in-the-world, is an ongoing effort to make life with knowledge of mortality liveable.

But let me point out that possession of knowledge, enabling as it is in so many crucial respects, cannot but disable in other respects – and so another grave reason is added to the necessity for the sociologist to critically engage with doxa. The job of knowledge – focusing human eyes and will on some fragments or aspects of the world – cannot be accomplished without 'collateral damage': diverting eyes and will from some other fragments or qualities. Such selectiveness of knowledge (the obstinate co-presence of disabling effects), and so also the mixed character of its blessings and the ambiguity of its impact, cannot be 'cured' – they are the necessary, non-negotiable conditions of the effectiveness of knowledge in their enabling capacity (the fulfilment of any task is facilitated by drawing a line cutting out the 'relevant' from the 'irrelevant': in other words, by the interplay of 'targeting on' and 'abstracting from').

Let me illustrate that unavoidable ambiguity and the resulting ambivalence by one, though by no means marginal and negligible, element of the present-day well-nigh universal worldview: the concept of 'risk' and 'risk calculation'.

Risk, as Ulrich Beck, the pioneer of its contemporary exploration and still its leading and most proficient theorist, points out, has 'amalgamate[d] knowledge with non-knowing within the semantic horizon of probability' from the beginning of modernity. The history of science, Beck claims, 'dates the birth of the probability calculus, the first attempt to bring the unpredictable under control – developed in the correspondence between Pierre Fermat and Blaise Pascal – to the year 1651'; and since then, through the category of risk, 'the arrogant assumption of controllability' has tended to increase in influence. With the benefit of hindsight, from the perspective of the admittedly liquidized sequel to an early modernity compulsively liquidizing yet solidity obsessed, we can say that the category of risk was an attempt to reconcile the two pillars of modern consciousness – an awareness of the contingency and randomness of the world on the one hand, and a 'we can' type of confidence on the other. More exactly, the category of 'risk' was an attempt to salvage the second, despite the obtrusive, resented and feared company of the first. The demand for the services that the categories of 'risk' and 'risk calculation' are capable of rendering grew in parallel with the accumulation of evidence of the essential, irrevocable and irreparable irregularity, contingency and indeterminacy of the world; the dream of an 'absolute' and 'eternal' extemporal truth and of an intractable regularity and law-abidingness of the world was, after all, the necessary premise for the modern ambition to act with certainty and self-confidence.

The accumulating evidence to the contrary, soon followed by scientifically theorized and mathematically substantiated models of an essentially underdetermined universe, put paid to such an ambition. The idea of risk was the second-best device to keep the search for truth on track – or a second line of trenches to which the modern desire for certainty was forced to withdraw. The category of 'risk' promised that even if the natural setting, as well as the human-made additions to that setting, were bound to stop short of unconditional regularity and so at a distance from the ideal of *a priori* transparency and complete predictability, human beings might still come quite close to the condition of certainty through gathering and storing knowledge and flexing its practical, technological arm. Unlike the now dashed hopes of full certainty and unimpaired confidence, the category of 'risk' does not promise foolproof security from dangers, but it does promise the ability to calculate their probability and likely volume – and so, obliquely, the possibility of calculating and applying the optimal distribution of resources to render intended undertakings effective and successful.

And yet ... Even if not explicitly, the semantics of 'risk' needs to assume, counterfactually yet axiomatically, a 'structured' ('structuring': manipulation and the resulting differentiation of probabilities), essentially rule-abiding and so in a sense regular and predictable environment: a universe in which the probabilities of events are predetermined, could be scrutinized, made known and assessed. Such an assumption being blatantly unsustainable, the 'calculation of risk' stratagem is nevertheless an attractive proposition: however short it might fall of the spiritual comfort offered by the promise of flawless and infallible certainty, as well as by the ensuing prospect of predetermining ('fixing') the future, that distance seems small and insignificant in comparison with the unbridgeable categorial abyss separating the 'semantic horizon of probability' (and so also the hoped-for calculation of risk) from the premonition of unmitigated and incurable uncertainty saturating and haunting contemporary liquid modern consciousness. In Jorge Wagensberg's summing up of the present-day scholarly wisdom (see his *L'âme de la méduse. Idées de la complexité du monde* (1997), p. 47), 'solutions (to equations) ramify, but only one solution is correct, only one represents the reality of a system. The problem is how to know which one. It is an accident that decides ... A minute fluctuation, hitherto negligible, now decides the future of a macroscopic system'. The complexity of systems in league with the uncertainty of their environments shift the right to the last word to fate: that cryptonym of a blend of the unpredictable and the uncontrollable. And as John Gray pointed out more than a dozen years ago, 'the governments of sovereign states do not know in advance how markets will react . . . National governments in the 1990s are flying blind.' Gray did not expect the future to usher us into markedly different conditions; as in the past, we could expect 'a succession of contingencies, catastrophes and occasional lapses into peace and civilization', all of them random, unexpected, unforeseeable and incalculable, catching their victims as well as their beneficiaries unawares and unprepared.

It seems ever more likely that the discovery and announcement of the centrality of a 'risk horizon' in modern consciousness has followed the eternal habit of the Owl of Minerva, known to spread its wings at the end of the day and just before nightfall, or the yet more common proclivity of objects, as noted by Martin Heidegger, to be transported from the state of 'hiding in the light', of being immersed in the obscure condition of *zuhanden*, to the dazzling visibility of *vorhanden*, no sooner than they go bust, are dropped from everyday life, or otherwise frustrate expectations – in other words, things burst into consciousness solely in their afterlife, and as a consequence of their disappearance or shocking trans-mogrification. Indeed, we became acutely conscious of the awesome role played by the categories of 'risk', 'risk calculation' and 'risk taking' in our modern history only at the moment when the term 'risk' had lost much of its former utility and needed to be used, as suggested by Jacques Derrida, *sous rature*, 'under erasure', having turned – to use Beck's own vocabulary – into a 'zombie concept'; when, in other words, the time had already arrived to replace the concept of *Risikogesellschaft* (risk society) with that of *Unsicherheitglobalschaft* (global uncertainty). Our dangers today differ from those the category of 'risk' strove to capture and bring to light, because they are unnamed before they strike, unpredictable and incalculable. And the setting in which our dangers are born and from which they emerge is no longer framed by the category of *Gesellschaft* – unless we deem the 'society', grossly prematurely, to be coterminous with the population of the planet itself.

What follows from all these lengthy considerations? That in lieu of or alongside its promised and assumed 'enabling' function, the idea of risk calculation and the strategic recommendations it implies may be performing a 'disabling' role. It draws our concerns, preoccupations and so also our efforts away from confronting point blank and in all its gravity and awesomeness the prospect of acting under conditions of perpetual and irremovable uncertainty and the need to acquire the skills and character rendered indispensable for such action.

Just a few examples of the uses about which you ask: the uses to which 'critique – and with it sociology' can, has to, and hopefully will be put in the years to come; years in which uncertainty looks set to be the only certainty we can count on . . .

In a piece entitled 'Critical theory' from 1991 you insisted on the nature of critical social theory that 'it will not be satisfied with the optimally faithful reproduction of the world "as it is". It will insist on asking, "how has this world come about?" It will demand that its history be studied, and that in the course of this historical study the forgotten hopes and lost chances of the past be retrieved. It will wish to explore how come that the hopes have been forgotten and the chances lost.' In the same piece, you also put it that, instead of being so preoccupied with the 'system's colonization of the lifeworld' (the famous Habermasian thesis), an equally important – perhaps even more pivotal – concern was with individualization, privatization and the disappearing or shrinking of arenas for public and political deliberation. Today, the agenda of critical social theory, according to your diagnosis, has thus changed quite considerably. What 'lost hopes and chances' should critical social theory particularly pay attention to, and is the main problem today still that proposed or prophesied 'colonization of the public by the private'?

I flatter myself, rightly or wrongly, that I remain loyal to this old postulate. Presently, I am preoccupied with surveying the paths leading to one grave and seminal departure, responsible more than any other recent developments for the growing and increasingly unbridgeable gap between the 'world as it is' and the world that 'could and should be': namely, the crisis of agency, of an answer to the harrowing question 'who is going to do it?'

The departure I have in mind here is the worrying separation and looming divorce between power (*Macht, pouvoir*), that is the ability to have things done, and politics, that is the ability to decide which things need to be done and which ones don't. Critical theory was free of such a worry in its youthful *Sturm und Drang* phase: such a divorce was all but inconceivable then (if its symptoms cropped up here and there, they could be dismissed as anomalies, temporary irritants soon to be repaired). Power and politics being the two necessary and sufficient conditions of effective action, and both in monopolistic possession of the state (in intention, if not practice), the answer to the question of 'who is going to do it' was crystal clear and self-evident to the point of non-contentiousness. No longer, though. Much of the power once contained in the sovereignty of the state has evaporated into Manuel Castell's global 'space of flows', whereas politics to this day stays local. It is now the question of 'who is going to do it' rather than the question of 'what to do' that saps critical imagination, impulse and vigour, while making any thinking and talking about the 'good society' look all but futile.

What followed that departure was the paradox of a progressive *collectivization of problems* coupled with the *privatization of the tools and means for their resolution*. A paradox left to the resolve of individuals, thereby charging them with the impossible task (note that, once enforced and unavoidable, tasks turn into a duty) of handling individually, on their own, challenges that are socially produced (and only socially resolvable). The result is something akin to buying family shelters in order to cope with an imminent nuclear war and to divert its impact from oneself.

Another consequence is the radical change in the 'morphology' of the social tissue; most seminally and spectacularly, the passage from the society of producers, in which critical theory spent its most exuberant, ebullient and fertile years, and beyond which the Frankfurt School hardly ever peeked, to a society of consumers. If the production/industrial settings that were expected to summon, contain, hold and accommodate the totality of humans were (by design or default) factories of solidarity, of the closing of ranks, and consequently the engines which recycled individual grievances into a collective interest and so also cemented individual actors into 'historical agents', the output of settings infested by consumerism and serving consumerism tends to be dispersion, isolation and exclusion. Little if any chance there for 'collective agents' of history able to play a role comparable to that most famously imputed to the 'proletariat', the archetype of producers condensing all the defining attributes of being-in-a-society-of-producers. The 'precariat' that is nowadays replacing the notion of the 'proletariat' as the generic name for the entirety of deprived, degraded, suffering and humiliated human beings is conspicuous for being unfit for that role; it is not a category in which present-day social critique hastens to invest its redemptive hopes. The aggregate that is baptized the 'precariat' is notable for replacing the sentiments of 'together we stand and together we fall' with those of 'each on his (her) own and the devil take the hindmost'. Not a soil in which solidarity, that adhesive that was once hoped to bind the solitary sufferers into historical agents, is likely to take root and thrive.

I would say that between them these three roads have brought us to the 'colonization of the public by the private'; in other words, the private has invaded and conquered the 'agora', that space in which it was expected and hoped that private interests would be translated into public issues, and public needs translated into private rights and duties.

Critical social theory has always claimed that society – the public – needs critical sociology and with it a critical reflexivity as a fish needs water in order to survive. Even

*if we agree that the public needs sociology, how could –
or should – we persuade the public that this is indeed
the case? Another way of posing this question is to do a
simple 'sociology of sociology'. If we live in a consumer
society, if we are all consumers nowadays, is sociology
just another product in the marketplace? And if it is, can
we sell anything without denying the very things we are
wanting to say?*

Yes, sociology is, as you put it, 'another product in the
marketplace' – and there is little left for the sociologist
to do except to draw the required conclusions or perpetually accept his or her own marginality and irrelevance;
and as you may gather from our conversation thus far,
choosing that latter option would amount, in my view,
to a betrayal of the sociologist's vocation. To recall Karl
Marx, like all other human beings, we sociologists may
be making history, but not under conditions of our own
choosing.

So yes, like other market goods, sociology needs to
'create clients' for the services it offers; in this society
of consumers, it is as a rule the offer that is expected
and obliged to create the demand, not vice versa. Some
products have a better chance of meeting such an obligation, whereas others have little or no chance of doing so;
this much depends on the 'conditions not of our choosing'. The rest, however (and this is quite a large 'rest'),
is fully a matter of, and fully depends on, our choices.
In finding quite an extensive and grateful audience, that
'rest' needs to be guided, again in my view, by one of the
principles engraved in gilded letters under the cupola of
Leeds Civic Hall, among the other canons of morality
which its funders and builders, pioneers of the industrial

revolution, believed should guide their labours in trying to change the world for the better: 'Honesty is the best policy.' In our case, 'honesty' translates, first and foremost, as the promise to stay honest to our sociological vocation and to deliver on that promise.

The promise in question is to sound the alarm whenever it is necessary to sound it. Even if the chance of that alarm being heard and listened to might be well-nigh non-existent. Take, for instance, what the great Polish thinker and poet Czesław Miłosz noted quite a few decades ago: 'The world strikes us as unreason incarnate, a product of some demented mind' – was that observation at the time Miłosz shared it with his readers a thought product unfit for mass consumption? An unsellable misfit? It might have seemed like that, especially seeing the reactions (or rather absence of reaction) of those people who accepted the 'official' TINA version of our shared existential condition, or at least accepted it as a certificate of safe conduct through the mire and the maze in which they were doomed to vegetate – or so they came to believe on the authority of the political leaders and mass media.

But the little booklet under the clarion-like title *Indignez-vous!* (in English as *Time for Outrage*) scripted in 2010 by the veteran French fighter turned statesman Stéphane Hessel, at ninety-three years old, has already sold millions of copies in twenty-seven languages, and brought millions of young and not-so-young Spaniards out on the streets in protest against a political system that failed to note the passing of its use-by date and was defending itself tooth and nail, by hook or by crook, against a demotion already disastrously overdue. And the message contained by that little book is as radical (and thus allegedly unsellable) as the messages only very few sociologists would dare to compose rather than dotting the 'i's and crossing the 't's on their research reports. In Hessel's own summary (and my translation):

> What currently happens in the world cannot be accepted. It needs to be changed. We know today as never before the true volume of the man-made devastation of our planet. That destruction has been going on for centuries. When will it end? We have no right to consent either to the monstrous misery cohabiting in close proximity to unimaginable wealth. And if we allow terrorism to develop further in the fashion in which it has grown in recent years, we are bound to find ourselves stood up against the wall.
>
> We must find a solution, but this little book does not offer it. This book needs to be viewed as an alert, a clarion call, an appeal to conscience, and a call to lift ourselves out of passivity and embrace responsibility for the fate of the world.

Alvin Ward Gouldner once stated that 'courtesy bites the tongue of critique'. Do we live in a society that is too courteous? Previously, you have compared the state of critique today with life at a camp site – something that is short-lived, non-committed and shallow. If critique were to become the opposite – aimed at long-term social conditions, committed and aiming at core concerns in society – how would this affect courteous society as we know it?

Perhaps I am blind and deaf, or perhaps the world has changed beyond recognition since Gouldner scribbled his verdict; or perhaps thresholds of civilized gentility have been radically lowered since – but 'courtesy' is one of the last words that would come to my mind were I asked to describe the world we live in. 'Hypocritical', yes; but to confuse hypocrisy (that is a, tendency to steer clear of what causes genuine pain and really makes people suffer, and to sell cruelty under the label of benevolence) with courtesy is after all hypocrisy's foremost objective and trademark strategy: 'political correctness' being one of its blatant, even if hypocritically disguised manifestations.

That 'world as we know it' is a caddish and boorish world. Bushes are no longer for beating about. If Victorians crammed piano legs into stockings, we put pianos on legs previously to be savoured only in the pages of pornographic magazines. We use daily, publicly and ostentatiously, a kind of language once confined to gutters and dens of vice. We no longer respect rights to privacy and intimacy. Maybe the Englishman's home is still his castle, but a castle open 24/7 to visitors, and inhabited by people fearing the absence or dearth of snooping onlookers as the most awesome of Egyptian plagues. We revel at the sight of the also-ran apprentices being shown the door, and of residents of Big Brother's house being voted out after a week-long string of routine humiliations and ridicule. We respect neither the dignity of others nor our own. When we hear the word 'honour', we reach for a dictionary (that is, in case we want to swot up for quizzes like *Who Wants to Be a Millionaire?* or *The Weakest Link*). And gratuitous mud-slinging (no longer punishable or, indeed, censured and condemned) has reached unprecedented heights of facility – courtesy (sic!) of protection offered by the anonymity, and so impunity, of internet calumny, slander and libel. It is as if the 'right to slander' has become the one human right most likely to be universally respected and defended tooth and nail by the agencies guarding the law.

Respect and (what follows!) trust are the two attributes of what used to be called 'civilized society' that are conspicuously missing from human interactions – whether conducted in private or put on public display. In fact, stripping individuals of respect and of the grounds to trust each other is in my view the paramount (and thus far astoundingly successful) stratagem in making the 'core concerns in society' (as you put it) off-limits to society's attention, care, action – and, indeed, concern . . .

I believe that it is respect for the humanity of another, and the right to be respected, that 'critique' needs to locate at the top or near the top of its agenda – if we wish it to stand a chance of reaching the (here I repeat after you once more) 'core concerns of society'. Without the resurrection of respect, there is no chance for solidarity. Without solidarity there is no chance of awaking the 'core concerns in society' from their present somnolence, and forcing them into the open out of the sealed shelter of human inattention.

Sociology – and the work of sociologists – is often criticized. The media present sociology as commonplaces hidden by jargon or as political platforming. Meanwhile, within academic departments, sociologists often review each other's books harshly. How should we respond to the critics?

How to respond? By doing our job well – that is, with the recipients/conversationalists constantly in view and an awareness of our own responsibility to and for them. Doing our job well does not necessarily mean working with our ears pricked for critical reactions, which given the multivocal and multifocal nature of the semantically loaded social space are bound to be mutually controversial; or above all for the pronouncements of 'peer reviewers' who, by the logic of their collective function, cannot but be concerned primarily with levelling their shared habitus *down* instead of *up*.

I repeat over and over again that the business of sociology is a continuous, unending and indeed two-sided conversation/exchange with 'common sense' construed by and invested into human experiences – and that means *with the rank and file practitioners of life*, not with the spokespeople for this or that profession, including our own; today, in our thoroughly deregulated, individualized age more than at any other stage in the history of sociology. In that conversation/exchange we appear in the dual role of teachers and pupils and we enter it knowingly with no upfront guarantee of being in the right. In order to be listened to and heard in that sort of exchange, one needs to learn the art of listening and hearing what is said. Practising our vocation requires a balanced blend of self-confidence and demureness. It also takes some courage: interpreting human experiences it is not the kind of life I would recommend to weathercocks.

Towards the end of The Sociological Imagination *(1959) C. Wright Mills claimed that the purpose of sociology is to improve the quality of human life. As you see it, is it the purpose of sociology to improve, enhance or make society/human life better, and if so, how?*

Through all its two centuries of history sociology has focused on the aspects of the human condition that derive from the fact that the human being is a 'social animal' – living in society, in the company of others, interacting with others, etc. – human 'sociality' being for sociologists the 'difference that made the difference'. Long before C. Wright Mills, Albion Small, one of the pioneers of sociology in the United States, pointed out that sociology was born of the desire to improve society – the tacit premise being Aristotle's proposition that the 'good life' is conceivable solely inside a good polis and that only beasts or angels can live without a polis. Want to do something about the quality of human life? Start by doing something about the quality of the society humans inhabit. There was, so to speak, a sort of 'elective affinity' between this understanding of the services sociology was bent on rendering and promising to render, and 'managerial reason' of the time, bent on making sure that desirable human actions would be forthcoming by manipulating their probability through the manipulation of the setting in which the actions were to take place – a manipulation calculated to limit, better still to eliminate altogether the actors' choices.

Managerial reason has since changed, along with the strategy of domination – shifting from an emphasis on 'hard power' (exacting discipline through coercion) to 'soft power' (relying on temptation and seduction). The idea of the 'good life' nowadays is cut away from the idea of the 'good society' and turned into a DIY job, a matter of individual concern and individual performance: no longer a question of 'improving society' but of finding or constructing a relatively comfortable niche in a hopelessly inhospitable social setting. The resulting radical change in the human condition confronts sociology with the need to rethink and recompose its vocation.

Does this recomposition mean that we need to look elsewhere than the time-honoured books and conferences if we want to communicate? Today, it has become increasingly popular for social critics, pundits and ordinary people to communicate their wisdom, voice their concerns, discuss contemporary issues or express their opinions via blogs on the internet. What does this say about the state of social debate today? Moreover, you do not seem to prefer this way of communicating your ideas. Why is this so?

I have been an irregular, yet frequent enough contributor to the sites of a few internet journals, particularly *Social Europe* in Britain and *Krytyka Polityczna* in Poland. But you are right, I do not prefer 'this way of communicating'. Perhaps it is a matter of age – too late to abandon or revise habits that have had more than enough time to gel and solidify. What I feel puts me off in blog-style communication, however, is the mind-boggling speed with which the messages enter and leave the realm of public attention – mostly intestate. They surf minds instead of settling inside them for the duration necessary for mature reflection and for their consequentiality. Quickly read, quickly forgotten. Communication on the internet is subject to the logic of fashion more than to that of debate. Flashes in the pan – not the way to make your roast well done . . .

Should sociologists – in their capacity as sociologists as well as private individuals – watch television and, if so, what should they see and why?

Watching TV is one of the sociologist's prime duties. It is there, in the world-as-seen-on-TV, that most people spend a good chunk of their lives and acquire a good chunk of their knowledge of the world. The *Lebenswelt*, the main object of our study and the main target of our messages, is sorely incomplete today if it is stripped of its online TV ingredients. Refusing to watch TV is tantamount to turning one's back on a considerable, and still growing part of contemporary human experience. This is the consideration that should guide and dictate the sociologist's selection of their viewing – rather than, regrettably, their aesthetic or other pleasure-seeking preferences. But who said that the work of sociologists must be – is bound to be – invariably pleasurable?